Catskill Country
COOKING

COMPILED BY **BEVERLY BORWICK**

WALKER AND COMPANY · NEW YORK

Royalties from the sale of this book will be
contributed to the Community General
Hospital of Sullivan County, Callicoon and
Harris, New York.

Second Edition

Published in the United States of America in 1976 by the Walker Publishing
Company, Inc.

Published simultaneously in Canada by Fitzhenry & Whiteside, Limited, Toronto.

ISBN: 0-8027-0528-6
Library of Congress Catalog Card Number: 75-15125
Printed in the United States of America.
10 9 8 7 6 5 4 3 2 1

With Appreciation

A great many individuals have contributed their talents to Catskill Country Cooking./ The Auxiliary of Community General Hospital is especially indebted to Professor Bruce Axler of the Hotel Technology Department of Sullivan County Community College for his overall guidance in the preparation of the book./ The recipes in this book have been reviewed by the staff of the Food Technology Department of Sullivan County Community College./

The committee is also thankful to Marge Smith and Bert Feldman for their assistance with the historical information for this book./ It takes many people working together to fulfill a project of this magnitude and we are grateful to all./ The "Cookbook Committee" itself consisted of the following individuals: Carla Kutsher: *Copy Editor,* Elaine Lewis Handy: *Art Direction and Design,* Harriet Finkelstein, Hazel Baum, Nathana Rosen, Betty Maythenyi, Eva Topal, Betty Foxman, Rebecca Rosenberg, Betty Fodor, Christine Yanello, Evelyn Haas, Ivy Blumenfeld, and Gloria Roche./

The committee could not have accomplished its goal without the support of the region's outstanding gourmets—individual hosts and hostesses, restaurateurs and hotel chefs—whose recipes appear in this publication, and others whose equally fine recipes must await our second edition because of lack of space in this one./

Beverly Borwick: *Chairperson*
Shirley Cohen: *Co-chairperson*

Sullivan County, N.Y.

The tradition of good eating and fine dining in the Sullivan County Catskills is intertwined with its history. It not only precedes our current luxury hotels, but goes back beyond the coming of white settlers to these regions.

First, of course, was the Indian who lived in a primitive relationship with the land and its yield. Inhabiting this country of forested hills, clear lakes, swift running streams and lushly fertile river floodplains, were the Lenni Lenape Tribe, also known as the Delawares. A rather unagressive people, partly agrarian, they lived both in towns along the river bottoms with well developed farms, or foraged for game and other delicacies in the forests. Their hunting camps became well established. The Yaugh Haus Spring, just north of Wurtsboro on Route 209, was a favorite gathering place.

In the agricultural settlements, the women prepared a variety of dishes based on cornmeal or coarse pounded corn, crushed either by a heavy stone tied to a sapling or against a hollowed tree trunk or ground in a primitive quern. A favorite dish was crushed corn mixed with berries and brought to a pudding-like consistency with added maple syrup and/or wild honey! The diet was varied with game, fish and shellfish, along with roast venison and other game, plus wild onions and succulent plants, both wild and domesticated. The Lenape lived a rich and healthy existence.

To this day, the berry crop growing wild everywhere is an outstanding feature of living in Sullivan County. Along the high ridges of the Shawangunks the blueberries are so abundant, that some families provide themselves with an extra income harvesting this wild delicacy.

In early May, the shad run in the upper Delaware River. Indescribably delicious, indescribably bony, the shad frightens off many fish gourmets. A local jingle says, *"When the Lord made shad/the devil was mad/for it seemed such a feast of delight./So to poison the scheme,/he jumped in the stream,/and stuck in the bones out of spite!"*

While the fish itself is a subject of debate, the shad roe is a treat that rivals caviar. *Shad Roe Meuniere,* with brown butter and the juice of a lime must be tasted to be believed.

Sullivan's waterways teem with fish of all kinds: brown, brook, lake and rainbow trout, large and small-mouth bass, perch, eels; the list goes on and on. In recent years, landlocked salmon have been introduced in certain parts of northern Sullivan. There are restaurants that maintain trout ponds where you may angle for the king of fresh water fish. What words can describe fish that fresh, just minutes out of the water?

Another exile returned to his original home is the wild turkey, once so abundant in these parts that a stream and a village have been named for him: Callicoon from the Dutch "kalkoen", the wild turkey. Served with wild rice, this bronze giant of a game bird far surpasses in taste his domesticated brethren.

Other game available to those who seek them include pheasant, quail, and deer, which, incidentally, makes a terrific sauerbraten.

As the county became settled, other ethnic groups found their way to the countryside. After the European revolutions of 1848, large numbers of Germans and Swiss settled the western sections of Sullivan, bringing hearty menus of *kartoffelpuffer* (potato pancakes), *klopse* (meatballs), rich pastries, *tortes,* and wonderful *würsts*.

In this area, there are restaurants specializing in such Teutonic treats, accompanied by steins of foaming lager.

In and around the Town of Lumberland are the settlements of Ukranians whose black bread, sour cream and cucumbers keep company with *holubtsi* (stuffed cabbage), *blintzi z syrom* (blinis with a difference), and other Slavic tantalizers.

Just before the First World War a new stream entered the Catskills. Fleeing from the czarist pogroms, large numbers of Jewish immigrants crowded the Lower East Side of New York City. Enterprising countrymen realizing their yearning for open space, green fields and trees made the 90 mile trip to buy old farms here, eventually transforming them into boarding-houses. From these erstwhile farms, grew the magnificent resorts of today. These new hotelkeepers served the freshest and finest, with a hand that was extravagently lavish and a pot that seemed bottomless. Certain traditions die hard, and newcomers to the Catskills marvel not only at the quality of the resort food, but also at the seemingly endless quantity.

In this book, we have endeavored to bring together some of that wonderful bounty that has assembled in this most unusual of places. You will find dishes that you would only expect to find in large, cosmopolitan cities. You will find some simple country cooking, and other dishes that are truly gourmet. Take a bite here, a nibble there, and forget the calories!

Contents

Appetizers

Ukrainian Fruit Cup With Wine

Serves 4

2 oranges
1 grapefruit
1 banana
1 pear
1 apple
½ cantaloupe
Juice of one lemon
½ cup sugar
½ cup wine (*sherry, port,*
  Muscatel or Tokay)

Peel fruit and cut into pieces./ Place fruit in a bowl, add lemon juice and sugar and mix well, taking care not to mash fruit./ Pour wine over all./ Let stand in refrigerator several hours, stirring once or twice./

Vegetarian "Chopped Liver"

Serves 6 to 8

1 lb. fresh green beans,
  snapped in 1 inch lengths
  (or 2-9 oz. packages frozen
  green beans,
  defrosted)
2 tbls. vegetable oil
1 lb. onions, diced
5 eggs, hard boiled
½ cup chopped walnuts
Salt
Pepper
1 tsp. mayonnaise (optional)
½ tsp. onion powder
  (optional)

If fresh green beans are used, cook in covered sauce pan in small amount of boiling salted water until beans are barely tender./ Drain beans./ Cook frozen beans as directed until barely tender and drain well./

Heat oil in skillet./ Sauté onions and beans in oil until onions are transparent but not brown./ In chopping bowl, place beans, onions, eggs and walnuts and chop ingredients until mixture is fine but not mushy./ Do not use blender or grinder./ Add salt and pepper to taste./ If mixture is too dry, add mayonnaise./ If additional onion flavor is desired, add onion powder./

Vegetarian "chopped liver" can be used as an appetizer on crackers or as a main dish with salad./

Vegetable-Cheese Spread

Yield: 2 pounds

4 stalks celery with leaves
3 medium carrots
1 small bunch radishes,
  unpeeled
1 medium cucumber,
  unpeeled
1 large green pepper, cored
  and seeded
1 medium onion
2 tbls. chopped parsley
1½ lbs. cream cheese,
  softened
Garlic powder
Salt

Wash and dry all vegetables./ With medium or fine blade of food grinder, grind all vegetables together, then drain in fine sieve, pressing with spoon./ With an electric mixer, beat cream cheese, add vegetables, garlic powder to taste and mix well./ Salt to taste./ Let spread ripen a few hours or overnight in refrigerator./

Serve as a sandwich filling or stuffing for tomatoes or green peppers./

Potato Knishes

Yield: 24 Knishes

4 cups flour
2 tsp. salt
1 tsp. baking powder
¾ cup vegetable shortening
Approximately ⅔ cup water
6 lbs. potatoes
2 cups onions, diced
¾ cup schmaltz (or butter or
  vegetable shortening)
1 cup eggs, beaten
1½ tsp. salt
¼ tsp. white pepper
Garlic powder
Egg wash (1 egg beaten with
  1 tbls. milk)

To make dough, combine flour, salt, and baking powder, then cut in shortening./ Lightly stir in enough water for dough to form a smooth, unsticky ball./ Divide dough into quarters./ On floured surface, roll out each quarter to form four 12 by 8 inch rectangles./

Peel potatoes and boil them until tender./ Drain and mash potatoes in mixer./ Sauté onions in schmaltz until golden and tender./ Mix sauteed onions with mashed potatoes, eggs, salt, pepper, and a pinch of garlic powder until well combined./ Divide filling into fourths./

Spoon each quarter of filling along the long side of a rectangle of dough./ Do not shape filling; leave some air space./ Lightly roll up filling in dough./ Repeat with remainder of filling and dough rectangles./

Place rolls on baking sheets./ Slash each roll at one inch intervals./ Brush with egg wash./ Bake knishes in a 400° F. oven for 45 minutes, or until golden./ Cut through each slash to make one inch slices./ Serve knishes hot or cold as an appetizer or side dish./

Seafood Dip

Yield: 2 pounds dip

14 to 15 oz. minced clams
½ lb. shrimp, cooked and
  peeled
½ lb. cream cheese
1½ tbls. prepared white
  horseradish
2 tsp. mayonnaise
Paprika
Onion salt
Garlic salt
Worcestershire sauce

In a bowl, combine clams, shrimp, cream cheese, horseradish, mayonnaise, dash of paprika, onion salt, garlic salt, and a few drops of Worcestershire sauce and grind in food grinder./ Chill the dip./

Serve dip with crisp crackers./

The Old Homestead Restaurant

Potato Peel Appetizer

Potato peels, from well-
  scrubbed potatoes
Coarse salt

In a shallow baking pan, arrange the peels./ Sprinkle them with coarse salt, and bake in a 350° F. oven for 45 minutes./

Party Chicken

Serves 8

⅓ cup honey
⅓ cup chili sauce
2 tbls. soy sauce
Dry mustard
1 large chicken, cut into
small pieces

In a saucepan, mix and heat honey, chili sauce, soy sauce, and a dash of dry mustard./ Dip pieces of chicken into mixture./
Cover bottom of a baking pan with aluminum foil, and place coated pieces of chicken in pan./ In a 350° F. oven, bake the chicken pieces for approximately 1½ hours./

Onion And Cheese Pie

Serves 6

1 unbaked 10" pie crust
½ lb. Swiss cheese, grated
2 tbls. flour
1 large onion, sliced
4 eggs, lightly beaten
1 cup heavy cream
1 cup milk
1 tsp. salt
½ tsp. curry powder
¼ tsp. nutmeg
Tabasco
Pepper

Mix grated cheese thoroughly with flour and spread in bottom of pie shell./ Separate onion slices into rings and arrange over cheese./ Beat together eggs, cream, milk, salt, curry powder, nutmeg, 2 drops of Tabasco, and freshly ground pepper to taste, and pour over onion rings./ Bake pie in a 350° F. oven for 45 minutes./
Pie can also be served as a luncheon dish with salad./

Shrimp Toast

Serves 6

½ lb. raw shrimp, shelled
and deveined
6 water chestnuts
1 egg, lightly beaten
1 tbls. scallions, finely
chopped
1 tbls. cornstarch
1 tsp. salt
1 tsp. ground ginger
1 tsp. sherry
½ tsp. sugar
6 slices firm white bread, at
least 2 days old
Peanut oil

Finely chop and mix shrimp and water chestnuts./ Add egg, scallions, cornstarch, salt, ginger, sherry, and sugar and mix until well blended./ Remove crust from bread, and cut each slice into 4 triangles./ Spread some of shrimp mixture on each piece./
In a large, heavy skillet, pour peanut oil to a depth of one inch and heat the skillet to 375° F./ Cook triangles, a few at a time, shrimp side down./ Cook until toast is light brown./ Drain shrimp toast on absorbent paper./ Serve hot./
Shrimp toast can be frozen and reheated in 350° F. oven for 10 to 15 minutes./

Old World Liptauer

Serves 4

½ cup butter (or ½ cup
   cottage cheese)
3 oz. cream cheese
1 small onion, chopped
   finely
1 tsp. prepared Dijon
   mustard
2 fillets of anchovy
   (or 1 generous tsp.
   anchovy paste)
½ tsp. paprika
Caraway seeds
Salt

Combine butter, cream cheese, onion, mustard, anchovy, paprika, a generous pinch of caraway seeds, and salt to taste in a bowl./ Blend mixture thoroughly with a fork./ Ripen Liptauer in the refrigerator overnight./

Serve Liptauer with thinly sliced dark pumpernickel or corn-rye bread./

Swiss Cheese Fondue

Serves 8

10 oz. imported Swiss cheese
10 oz. Swiss Gruyère cheese
1 clove garlic, cut in half
1⅔ cups good white wine
2 tsp. cornstarch
1 to 1½ tbls. Kirsch brandy
1 to 1½ loaves French bread,
   cut into large bite-sized
   cubes

Grate cheese./ Rub the inside of fondue pot with cut edges of garlic./ Add wine and cheese to the fondue pot, and heat the mixture on a medium heat./ With a flat wooden spoon, stir mixture constantly until cheese starts to melt, and then stir in figure eight motions./ When the mixture bubbles, lower heat to simmer./

Mix cornstarch with Kirsch, and add to the fondue pot./ Simmer for a minute or two./ If the mixture does not thicken, add additional cornstarch mixed with water./

Place the fondue on an alcohol burner with low heat./ Serve fondue by placing bread cube on a long-handled fork, and dipping the cube into the fondue, again stirring in a figure eight./ The fondue will become thicker as it sits./

Shrimp Filling For Celery

Yield: ¾ cup

5 oz. can shrimp, drained
   and chopped
⅓ cup mayonnaise
¼ cup crushed pineapple
1 tbls. nuts, chopped
2 tsp. parsley, chopped
1½ tsp. lemon juice
1½ tsp. onion, chopped
¼ tsp. salt
Tabasco

In a bowl, mix shrimp, mayonnaise, pineapple, nuts, parsley, lemon juice, onion, salt, and a dash of tabasco./ Chill the mixture./ Stuff celery with the shrimp filling./

Ukrainian Pickled Herring

Serves 24

12 herrings
2 onions, sliced thinly
1 lemon, sliced thinly
2 pints vinegar
2 bay leaves
1 tsp. salt
½ tsp. pepper
2 cloves
¼ tsp. allspice
¼ tsp. cinnamon
¼ tsp. mace
1 tbls. olive oil

In a bowl, soak herring for 3 hours in cold water./ Drain and remove skin and bones from fish./ Cut herring into fillets lengthwise and layer in a jar with onion and lemon slices between./ In a saucepan, combine vinegar, bay leaves, salt, pepper, cloves, allspice, cinnamon and mace and bring to a boil./ Cool vinegar mixture, add oil to it and pour over herring./ Cover jar and store in a cool place for 2 weeks before serving./

Sulze (Head Cheese)

Serves 24

1 pig's head
Water
3 to 4 tbls. salt
3 to 4 lbs. pork shoulder
4 onions
1 stalk celery
½ cup white vinegar
8 or 9 peppercorns
1 large bay leaf
1 tsp. whole allspice
½ tsp. dried thyme
6 dill pickles, peeled and
  diced
1-6 oz. can pimentos,
  drained and diced
White pepper

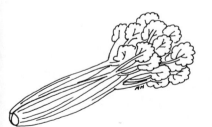

Scrub pig's head thoroughly, rinse and drain./ In a large bowl, place pig's head and cover with water to which 2 or 3 tablespoons of salt has been added./ Cover bowl and refrigerate overnight./

The following day, drain pig's head and rinse./ In a very large pot, place pig's head and pork shoulder with water to cover./ Add 2 onions cut in half, celery, vinegar, one tablespoon salt, peppercorns, bay leaf, allspice and thyme./ Bring to a boil, lower heat, skim fat from surface and simmer until meat is tender, approximately 2 hours./ Remove pot from heat and allow contents to cool./ Discard spices, reserving stock./ Cut all meat off the bones, dicing in ½ inch squares./ Peel and dice remaining 2 onions./ In a bowl, combine diced meat with dill pickles, pimento and diced onions./ Heat stock (if stock does not have enough body, reduce it over medium heat), add meat mixture and season with salt and white pepper to taste./ Bring mixture to a boil, then pour into a mold or loaf pan and let cool./ Stir while mixture is jelling./ When firmly jelled, invert mold and cut head cheese into ½ inch slices./ Serve with vinaigrette sauce./

Reber's Restaurant

Eggs-Tremely Good Dip

Yield: 2 cups

½ cup mayonnaise
1½ tbls. lemon juice
1 tbls. onion juice
2 tsp. prepared mustard
½ tsp. Tabasco
½ tsp. seasoned salt
¼ tsp. white pepper
6 eggs, hard-boiled
4 oz. whipped cream
  cheese with pimento,
  softened
Parsley

In a mixer or blender, combine mayonnaise, lemon juice, onion juice, mustard, tabasco, salt, and pepper./ Add eggs, one at a time, beating the mixture after each addition until it is smooth and light./ Beat cream cheese into the mixture./ Spoon the dip into a bowl and garnish with parsley sprigs./ Serve dip with chips and crackers or raw vegetable sticks./

Chopped Liver

Serves 6

1 large slice beef liver
¼ cup chicken fat
2 large onions, diced
3 eggs, hard boiled
1 heaping tbls. mayonnaise
  (optional)
1 tsp. honey
Salt
Pepper

In a skillet, fry liver in 2 tablespoons chicken fat for 5 minutes./ Add diced onions and sauté the ingredients until the onions are golden-brown and the liver cooked through./

In a large chopping bowl, mash hard-boiled eggs finely, and add mayonnaise to the eggs if desired./ Add liver, onions, and pan scrapings to eggs; chop mixture finely./ Add remaining fat, honey, salt and pepper to taste to the chopped liver and mix well./

Tomato Quiche

Serves 12

2 unbaked 9″ pie crusts
Beaten egg white
4 eggs
1½ cups milk
½ cup evaporated milk
2 tbls. butter, melted
½ tsp. salt
⅛ tsp. nutmeg
Cayenne
3 to 4 slices bacon, cooked,
  drained and crumbled
1-20 oz. can salad-type
  tomatoes
1 cup Gruyère or Swiss
  cheese, grated

Brush pie crusts with beaten egg white and place in refrigerator until dry./ (This seals the crust and prevents the filling from soaking in.)/

In a large bowl, beat eggs with milk, evaporated milk, melted butter, salt, nutmeg and a dash of cayenne./ Divide crumbled bacon and spread over bottom of pie crusts./ Drain tomatoes and arrange evenly over bacon./ Sprinkle cheese over tomatoes./ Pour egg mixture over tomatoes and place in a preheated 400° F. oven./ Reduce heat to 375° F. and bake 35 to 40 minutes, or until a toothpick inserted in the center comes out clean./ Let quiche cool for 15 minutes before serving./

Tahina (Sesame Paste Appetizer)

Serves 8

5¼ oz. sesame seeds
1 cup water
Juice of 2 lemons
2 cloves garlic
1 tsp. salt
Cayenne
3 tbls. olive oil
3 tbls. parsley, chopped
Paprika
Olives

Place sesame seeds, water, lemon juice and garlic in blender and blend until pasty./ Add more water if necessary to achieve a mayonnaise-like consistency./ Add salt and pinch of cayenne./ Serve flattened on little plates, garnished with a swirl of olive oil, a sprinkling of parsley and paprika and centered with olives./

Tahina may be diluted with vinegar and used as a salad dressing or sauce./ Without the garnishes, it can serve as a cocktail dip./

Sardine Dip

Serves 6

1 can skinless and boneless
  sardines
4 oz. cream cheese, room
  temperature
1 tbls. grated onion (or onion
  juice)
1 tsp. lemon juice
½ tsp. Worcestershire sauce

Drain sardines, then mash them./ In a bowl, cream the cream cheese until light and fluffy./ Blend sardines with cream cheese./ Add onion, lemon juice, and Worcestershire sauce and mix well./

Serve dip with chips and crackers./

Romanian Eggplant Caviar

Serves 4 to 6

1 to 1½ lb. eggplant
Oil
½ green pepper
1 small onion, chopped fine
2 tbls. oil
1 tbls. cider vinegar

Oil skin of eggplant./ Place uncovered eggplant on oven tray./ In a 350° F. oven, bake eggplant until soft, turning it several times./

Split eggplant and scoop out insides, discarding skin./ Chop eggplant with green pepper until smooth./ Chill the mixture./ At serving time, add the onion, oil, and vinegar to the eggplant mixture./

Hot Crab Meat Dip

Serves 4 to 6

8 oz. cream cheese
7½ oz. frozen King crab
2 tbls. dry sherry
1 tsp. lemon juice
8 oz. slivered unblanched
  almonds

In a blender, mix cream cheese, crab, sherry, and lemon juice./ Place the mixture in a small casserole and cover it with almonds./ Cover the casserole and bake it in a preheated 350° F. oven for 25 minutes or until the mixture bubbles./

Serve dip with crisp crackers./

The Old Homestead Restaurant

Russian Mushroom Caviar

Serves 4

1 cup onions, chopped
⅓ cup butter or margarine
1 tsp. paprika
2 cups fresh mushrooms,
  chopped
2 tbls. wine vinegar
Salt
Pepper
⅔ cup sour cream
⅓ cup fresh dill or parsley,
  chopped
2 tbls. chives or green
  onions, chopped

In a skillet, sauté the onions in butter until tender./ Stir in paprika and cook one minute./ Add mushrooms, vinegar, salt and pepper to taste and continue cooking for 4 minutes./ Stir in sour cream and dill or parsley and heat through over low heat./ Sprinkle with chopped chives or green onions and serve with black bread or pumpernickel./

Hommus (Bean Appetizer)

Yield: 3½ cups

1 lb. dried chick peas (or
  canned chick peas,
  drained)
Water
1 cup sesame seed (or
  peanut) oil
1 clove garlic, minced
4 tbls. lemon juice
1 tsp. salt
⅛ tsp. cayenne pepper
Salt
Pepper

Wash the chick peas, and place them in a pot with water to cover./ Bring water to a boil./ Remove pot from heat and let peas soak one hour./ Drain the peas and add fresh water to cover./ Cook the peas on medium heat for approximately two hours or until they are very soft./ Drain again./

Combine chick peas with oil, garlic, lemon juice, salt, and cayenne pepper in a bowl./ Mash the mixture until it is very smooth./ Season the hommus with salt and pepper to taste, and chill it well./ Serve the hommus as a spread with crisp crackers./

Chopped Herring

Serves 6

4 salt herring fillets
½ cup tart apple, finely
  chopped
2 eggs, hard-boiled, finely
  chopped
1 ½ tbls. onion, finely
  chopped
3 tbls. cider vinegar
2 tbls. salad oil
1 tsp. sugar
2 slices white bread, trimmed
Salt
Pepper

Soak the herring for 12 hours, changing the water at least twice./ Drain herring and then chop it as finely as possible./ Combine herring with apple, eggs, and onion./

Beat vinegar with oil and sugar./ Pour vinegar mixture over white bread, allowing it to soak in for a few minutes./ Add soaked bread to herring mixture, and chop them together until smooth./ Season with salt and pepper to taste and chill./

Falafel Appetizer

Yield: 75 croquettes

1 lb. dried chick peas
1 large onion
2 cloves garlic
2 or 3 sprigs parsley
1 tbls. cumin
Salt
Pepper
Paprika
Matzo meal
Peanut oil

Soak peas overnight, or approximately 12 hours, in cold water./ Drain peas, remove skins, and grind peas with onion, garlic, and parsley./ Add cumin, and salt, pepper and paprika to taste./ Mix ingredients until well blended./ If mixture is too wet, add a little matzo meal./ Refrigerate for 2 to 3 hours./

In a deep pan, heat approximately 2 inches of oil./ Scoop up chick pea mixture in rounded tablespoons, forming into balls, and lower into hot oil./ Cook only one layer at a time./ Fry balls until cooked through and brown, checking that centers are no longer soft./ With slotted spoon, lift out cooked croquettes and drain on paper towels./

Falafel Sauce

½ cup lemon juice
½ cup water
2½ oz. sesame seeds
1½ cloves garlic
1 tsp. salt
1 sprig parsley

Put all ingredients through a blender./ Sauce should turn pale and thin./

Falafel Salad

Shredded lettuce
Tomatoes, sliced
Cucumber, diced
Green pepper, diced
Radishes, sliced
Scallions, cut into small
  pieces
Oil
Vinegar
Salt
Pepper

In a bowl, place salad vegetables./ Combine 3 parts oil to one part vinegar, adding salt and pepper to taste, and whip dressing until heavy and white./ Toss salad with dressing and mix well./

Falafel Assembly:
Serve falafel as a snack or appetizer./ As an appetizer, place 3 or 4 falafel covered with sauce and salad inside pita bread./ For a late supper snack, serve 7 to 8 falafel./

Instant Pizza
Serves 6 to 8

3 cups buttermilk baking mix
½ to ¾ cup milk
1 to 2 tbls. olive oil
1¼ cups Italian tomato
  sauce
1 medium onion, chopped
½ can anchovies, drained
  and chopped
½ lb. pepperoni, thinly
  sliced
½ cup grated Romano
  cheese

Place buttermilk baking mix in a bowl and gradually add milk, mixing with a large spoon, until a soft dough is formed./ Turn out on floured board./ Knead dough until smooth, 8 to 10 times./ Place dough on a baking sheet and roll out to fit pan./

Brush dough with olive oil./ Spread tomato sauce on top of dough, and cover with onion, anchovies, pepperoni, and cheese./ In a 400° F. oven, bake pizza for 15 to 20 minutes./

Seafood Cocktail With Dubonnet Sauce
Serves 10 to 12

2 lbs. halibut
Juice of 2 lemons
3 bay leaves
1 tbls. salt
1 tsp. sugar
1-12 oz. bottle chili sauce
2 tbls. white prepared
  horseradish
2 tbls. Dubonnet
½ tsp. oregano
1 tsp. capers, chopped
  (optional)

In a large saucepan, place fish with water to cover./ Add lemon juice, bay leaves, salt and sugar and bring to boil./ Reduce heat and simmer for 20 minutes./ Cool fish in liquid./ Remove fish, discard skin and bones, and flake fish./

In a bowl, blend chili sauce, horseradish, Dubonnet, oregano and capers./ Mound fish onto serving platter on bed of lettuce and pour sauce over./ Serve with lemon wedges./

Herring In Cream Sauce
Serves 12

6 whole schmaltz herring
Cold water
4 cups white vinegar
1 cup and 1 tbls. sugar
4 bay leaves
1 tbls. mixed pickling spices
4 onions, thinly sliced
2 cups sour cream

In a large bowl, soak herring in cold water, refrigerated, for 2 days, changing the water twice during the process./ Remove herring, reserving water, and fillet, skin and bone it./ Cut fillets into 2 inch pieces and place in a large bowl./

In a saucepan, combine reserved water, vinegar, one cup sugar, bay leaves and pickling spices, bring to a boil and simmer for 10 minutes./ Cool and strain, then pour brine over herring, cover bowl and refrigerate for 48 hours./ Drain herring./ Blend together onions, sour cream and remaining one tablespoon sugar./ Combine herring and sour cream mixture and place in a glass container./ Refrigerate, covered, for 48 hours before serving./ Serve on a bed of lettuce with tomato wedges./

Chef: Frank Stubite   *Concord Hotel*

Soups

Beef Soup With Liver Dumplings

Serves 8 to 10

4 large marrow bones
1 carrot
1 parsnip
1 stalk celery
1 whole onion
5 whole black peppercorns
5 whole white peppercorns
3 whole allspice
Salt
2 to 2½ quarts cold water
Vegetable Bouillon

In a large pot, place marrow bones, carrot, parsnip, celery, onion, peppercorns, allspice, and salt to taste./ Add 2 to 2½ quarts cold water to pot./ Boil the mixture 1 to 1½ hours, and then strain it./ Season the soup to taste by adding a packet of vegetable bouillon./

Liver Dumplings

½ lb. chicken liver, scraped
  or ground
1 egg
1 clove garlic, smashed and
  minced
½ cup bread crumbs
  (*additional bread crumbs
  may be required*)
1 tbls. farina
1 tsp. parsley, chopped
Salt
Pepper

Combine all ingredients, including salt and pepper to taste, and beat till smooth./ If mixture is too soft to hold shape on a spoon, beat additional bread crumbs into it./

Wet soup spoon in soup, form dumpling on spoon from mixture, and drop it into boiling soup./ If dumplings do not stay together when dropped into soup, add bread crumbs to further bind mixture./ Boil dumplings in soup 7 to 10 minutes./ Serve soup with 2 to 3 dumplings per person./

Slavia Mt. Resort

Beet Borscht

Serves 8

1-16 oz. can whole beets
Water
Juice of ½ lemon
2 eggs
2 tbls. cold water
1 tbls. salt
Pepper
2 tbls. sugar
Sour cream (*optional*)

In a large pot, pour liquid from can of beets./ Leaving beets in can, fill can with water four times, each time adding water to pot./ Reserve beets./ Add lemon juice to pot, and bring liquid to a fast boil./

In a large bowl, beat eggs with cold water, salt, and a dash of pepper./ Gradually add small amounts of hot borscht to the foamy egg mixture./ Beat the mixture quickly and continually, until most or all the borscht is mixed in./

Quickly return hot borscht mixture to the large pot, and immediately pour the borscht back into the bowl./ Repeat this transfer process 6 to 8 times, ending with borscht in pot./ Add sugar to borscht./ Grate beets and add them to pot./

Allow the borscht to cool./ When serving, add a dollop of sour cream to individual bowls, if desired./

Vegetable Beef Soup

Serves 8

3 lbs. beef shank
1-33 oz. can tomato juice
7 cups water
⅓ cup onion, chopped
4 tsp. salt
2 tsp. Worcestershire sauce
¼ tsp. chili powder
2 bay leaves
1 lb. canned tomatoes
1 cup celery, diced
1 package frozen corn
1 package frozen green beans
1 cup carrots, diced
1 cup potatoes, diced
1 package frozen lima beans
  (*optional*)

In a large pot, combine meat, tomato juice, water, onions, salt, Worcestershire sauce, chili powder, and bay leaves./ Cover pot and simmer soup for approximately 2½ hours or until meat is tender./

Cut meat from bones into small chunks./ Add tomatoes, celery, corn, beans, carrots, potatoes, and lima beans, if desired, to soup, and simmer an additional hour./

Venison Vegetable Soup

Serves 20

6 to 8 quarts water
2 or 3 large venison bones
1 lb. venison meat
5 tsp. salt
6 stalks celery
3 large onions
Pepper
1-28 oz. can tomatoes
1 cup carrots, finely chopped

In a Dutch oven, soak venison bones and meat overnight in water with 3 teaspoons salt./ Drain./ Place bones, meat, 3 stalks of celery, 2 onions, 2 teaspoons salt and pepper to taste in a 10 quart pot and simmer on low heat for 4 to 5 hours, until meat falls off bones./ Remove and discard vegetables and bones./ Chop meat and reserve./

Finely chop one cup each of celery and onions./ Add vegetables to broth./ Add tomatoes and chopped carrots and cook until vegetables are tender./ Return meat to soup./ Skim fat, heat meat through and serve./

Peanut Soup

Serves 3

2 tbls. onion, minced
1 tbls. butter (*or margarine*)
¼ cup peanut butter
1 can cream of chicken soup
1 soup can of water
¼ cup milk
Parsley, minced (*or carrot,
  grated or bacon bits*)

In a saucepan, sauté onion in melted butter until tender./ Blend in peanut butter./ Add soup, water, and milk to mixture./ Heat, stirring ingredients occasionally./ Garnish with parsley, carrot, or bacon bits./

Czechoslovakian Potato Soup
Serves 8

7 cups water
3 potatoes, peeled and diced
2 tbls. dried mushrooms
½ cup each of mixed
  vegetables (shredded
  cabbage, chopped
  cauliflower, sliced carrots,
  diced celery, diced onions,
  substitute if desired)
1 tbls. salt
1 clove garlic, crushed
6 tbls. sweet butter
1 cup flour
2 tbls. cold water
Green parsley (or chives),
  chopped

Boil water in a large pot./ Add potatoes and mushrooms to boiling water, then add mixed vegetables./ Boil soup until all vegetables are tender./ Add salt and garlic to the soup./
In a saucepan, melt butter over low heat, gradually adding flour and stirring until flour is golden./ Cool./ When mixture is cool, add cold water, stir, and pour into boiling soup./ Simmer soup for five minutes./ When serving, add green parsley or chives to soup./

Corn Soup
Serves 2

1 small onion, chopped
1 stalk celery, chopped
2 tbls. butter (or margarine)
1 cup canned
  whole kernel corn
1 cup milk
3 tbls. grated Parmesan
  cheese
¼ cup tomato purée (or
  sauce)
Salt
Pepper
Tabasco (optional)

In a skillet, sauté onions and celery in butter./ Blend corn and milk in blender, leaving some kernals whole./ In a large saucepan, combine these two mixtures with cheese, tomato purée, and salt, pepper, and tabasco, if desired, to taste./ Cook soup until hot./

Cold Yogurt Soup
Serves 4

1 lb. small cucumbers,
  peeled and diced
Salt
3 cups yogurt
Olive oil
Dill, chopped
8 very large cloves of garlic,
  crushed
Mint (optional)

In a colander, place cucumbers and sprinkle them with salt./ Allow cucumbers to drain for approximately ½ hour./
In a bowl, place yogurt and add cucumbers, a few drops of olive oil, a generous sprinkle of dill, and crushed garlic and mix well./ If consistency of soup is too thick, add some water to thin it./ Refrigerate soup for 24 hours before serving./ When serving, sprinkle soup with dill or mint, if desired./

Steve's Legal* Soup

Serves 8

Vegetable oil spray
1 cup onions, thinly sliced
1 cup carrots, diced
1 cup celery, diced
2 cups zucchini, diced
1 cup green beans, diced
3 cups cabbage, shredded
6 cups homemade broth (or
  2 cups canned beef broth
  mixed with 4 cups water)
Crust from a 1 lb. piece of
  Parmesan cheese, scraped
  clean
2 to 3 cups canned Italian
  tomatoes, undrained
1 tbls. salt
Tabasco
½ cup grated Parmesan
  cheese
Salt
Pepper

In a large saucepan sprayed with vegetable oil coating, sauté onions for 5 minutes./ Add carrots to pan, cooking them 2 to 3 minutes, stirring once or twice./ Repeat 3 times, adding celery, zucchini, and green beans to pan, cooking them 2 to 3 minutes and stirring once or twice./ Add cabbage and cook mixture for 6 minutes, stirring occasionally./

Add broth, cheese crust, tomatoes with juice, salt and tabasco to taste./ Cover saucepan and cook soup at slow boil for 3 hours./

Before removing saucepan from heat, remove cheese crust./ Swirl grated cheese into soup./ Season with salt and pepper to taste./

*Legal: to Weight Watchers

Schav Soup

Serves 8

1 lb. schav (*sour grass*)
2 quarts water
2 tsp. salt
2 eggs
Juice of one lemon

Wash leaves, remove tough stems, and shred./ In a large saucepan, boil leaves in salted water for 10 minutes./ Cool mixture./ In a bowl, beat eggs, beat in lemon juice, then mix in schav./ Add more salt if desired./ Refrigerate soup until serving./ Serve cold with dollops of sour cream./

Blueberry Soup

Serves 10 as a soup-20 as punch

2½ quarts water
4 cups blueberries
½ cup sugar
Thin peel of one lemon
½ rind of tangerine
  (*optional*)
2 tbls. cornstarch
¼ cup cold water

Place 2½ quarts water in a large saucepan and simmer blueberries, sugar, lemon rind and tangerine rind, if desired, until berries are soft./ Strain, reserving liquid, and press berries through a sieve or puree in a food mill./ Return fruit to strained liquid./ Add cornstarch mixed with cold water to saucepan and simmer 5 minutes./

Chill thoroughly and serve with sweetened whipped cream dusted lightly with cinnamon./

Corn Chowder

Serves 4 to 6

¼ lb. salt pork, diced
1 tbls. onion, minced
1 tbls. green pepper, minced
1 tbls. celery, minced
2 cups fresh uncooked
   corn kernels
2 cups chicken broth
2 cups light cream
1 cup potato, cooked and
   diced
Salt
Pepper

Cook diced salt pork in a large saucepan until pork is crisp and brown./ Remove bits of pork and set them aside./ Add onion, green pepper, and celery to the salt pork fat and cook for 5 minutes over low heat, stirring frequently./ Add corn and chicken broth to the mixture, and simmer chowder 5 minutes./ Add cream and potato to the chowder, and heat it to a boil./ Add salt and pepper to taste./ Serve chowder with crisp pork bits./

Mushroom Soup

Serves 8

7 chicken bouillon cubes in
   7 cups water (or 7 cups
   chicken broth)
1 cup fresh mushrooms,
   sliced
1 medium yellow onion,
   diced
1½ tbls. butter
1 tbls. flour
1 tbls. rice
1 bay leaf
Salt
Pepper
Watercress (or parsley)

In a large saucepan, combine first seven ingredients./ Add salt and pepper to taste./ Bring soup to a boil, then lower heat and let soup simmer for one hour./ Remove bay leaf from soup and serve topped with watercress or parsley./

Cold Fruit Soup

Serves 6

1 cup peach juice, drained
   from canned peaches
1 cup pear juice, drained
   from canned pears
1 cup apricot juice, drained
   from canned apricots
1 cup cherry juice, drained
   from canned cherries
1 cup sour cream
1 cup fruit cocktail, drained
1 tsp. sugar
1 tsp. grenadine

In large bowl, whip peach, pear, apricot, and cherry juices with sour cream./ Add fruit cocktail, sugar, and grenadine to bowl, and mix well./ Chill the soup before serving./

Chef: Oscar Tomcykoski   *Gilbert's Hotel*

Pasta E Fagioli

Serves 10

2 tbls. olive oil
2 tbls. parsley, chopped
2 cloves garlic
2 quarts meat stock or water
1-6 oz. can tomato paste
1 tsp. basil
Salt
Pepper
1 lb. Italian hot or sweet
  sausage
1-20 oz. can Mexican chick
  peas
1-20 oz. can cannellini
  (white kidney beans)
2 stalks celery, chopped
1 large onion, chopped
1 cup ditalini macaroni
1 small zucchini, thinly
  sliced
Romano or Parmesan cheese,
  grated

In a large pot, sauté parsley and garlic in olive oil./ Add stock or water, tomato paste, basil and salt and pepper to taste and simmer./ In a frying pan, brown sausage slowly to remove excess fat./ (Link sausage can be simmered in a small amount of water for 10 minutes.)/ Slice sausage thinly./ To soup base, add sausage, undrained cans of chick peas and cannellini, celery and onion and heat to boil./ Add ditalini./ Cook, uncovered, till pasta is almost done./ Add zucchini./ Continue to simmer until zucchini is tender but still firm./ Serve soup with grated cheese./

Goulash Soup

Serves 6

½ lb. onions, chopped
¼ lb. bacon, diced
1 tsp. paprika
½ tsp. caraway seeds
1 clove garlic, crushed
Marjoram
6 cups beef stock
  (additional beef stock
  may be required)
1 lb. soup meat, finely cubed
1 tsp. salt
3 large tomatoes, peeled,
  seeded, and diced
¾ lb. potatoes, peeled
  and diced
¼ cup flour
¾ cup water
3 cooked beef frankfurters,
  peeled & cut in ¼" slices
Lemon

In a large saucepan, sauté onions with bacon until onions are golden./ Add paprika, caraway seeds, a pinch of marjoram, and garlic and cook for one minute, stirring./ Add stock, meat, salt, and tomatoes to saucepan, and simmer soup for 20 minutes./

Add potatoes and more beef stock, if necessary, to the soup./ Continue cooking soup until potatoes are soft./ Stir flour into water, and add this mixture slowly to soup./ Continue cooking until soup is thickened./ Add frankfurter slices and a squeeze of lemon./

Hominy Soup

Serves 6

1½ lbs. pork (*sides, hocks,*
  or stew meat)
32 oz. hominy
16 oz. pinto beans (*or red*
  kidney beans)
3 to 4 cups water
Salt
Pepper

In a large saucepan, brown meat./ Add hominy, beans and water to saucepan, with salt and pepper to taste./ Cook soup over low heat 1 to 2 hours./

Old Fashioned Manhattan Clam Chowder

Serves 12

¼ lb. salt pork, diced
2 onions, finely chopped
4 potatoes, peeled and diced
2 stalks celery with leaves,
  finely chopped
2 large carrots, peeled and
  diced finely
1 cup corn kernels
3 cups clam broth
3 cups canned tomatoes
2 tbls. tomato paste
1 tsp. salt
¼ tsp. pepper, freshly
  ground
3 cups canned chopped
  clams, drained
½ tsp. dried thyme

In a large skillet, sauté salt pork until it is crisp and lightly browned./ Add onions to skillet and sauté them until they are transparent but not browned./ Add potatoes, celery, carrots, corn, clam broth, tomatoes, tomato paste, salt, and pepper to the skillet./

Bring the mixture to a boil, cover the skillet, and simmer soup for approximately 15 minutes, until potatoes are barely tender./ Add chopped clams and thyme to the chowder./ Recover the skillet and cook 5 minutes longer./

Lefty's Charbroil

Lentil Soup

Serves 8

1 large onion, diced
1 large carrot, diced
2 stalks celery with leaves,
  diced
2 tbls. butter
1 lb. lentils, soaked overnight
  if necessary
2 tbls. flour
1 quart and 1 cup ham or
  beef stock
2 medium potatoes, peeled
  and diced
12 frankfurters, boiled and
  sliced

In a Dutch oven, saute onion, carrot and celery in butter for 15 minutes./ Mix lentils and flour together and add to mixture./ Add ham or beef stock and potatoes and continue cooking until all vegetables are tender./ Add frankfurters and serve at once./

Yellow Split Pea Soup

Serves 8 to 12

1 carrot, diced
1 stalk celery, diced
1 onion, diced
3 tbls. butter or margarine
1 tbls. flour
1 lb. yellow split peas,
  soaked overnight if
  necessary
3 quarts water
Salt
Pepper

In a Dutch oven, saute carrot, celery and onion in butter till tender./ Stir in flour./ Add peas and water./ Cook over low heat until peas are tender./ Season with salt and pepper to taste./

Chef: Willie Thomas   Kutsher's Country Club

Fish and Shellfish

Lobster Fra Diablo

Serves 2

1-1½ lb. lobster
Flour
2 tbls. olive oil
1 large clove garlic, minced
Oregano
¼ cup wine (sherry)
1-28 oz. can peeled tomatoes
  (Italian Plum)
6 littleneck clams
2 cups prepared tomato
  sauce
¼ tsp. crushed red pepper
Parsley, chopped

Remove claws from lobster and crack shells lightly./ Split the lobster in half, up the middle of the underside, and remove the sack./ Flour the meat side lightly./

In a heavy skillet, heat oil and add garlic and a pinch of oregano./ When the aroma becomes apparent, add wine and lobster, meat side down./ Crush the peeled tomatoes over the lobster, adding the juice from the can to the skillet./ Turn the lobster over, shell side down, and add the claws, clams, tomato sauce, and red pepper, mixing and basting the lobster occasionally with sauce./ Reduce heat and simmer until clams open./

Garnish with chopped parsley./

Bernie's Holiday Restaurant

Quenelles De Chateau

Serves 4

Quenelles
1 lb. pike, boned
Ground nutmeg
Cayenne pepper
Salt
Black pepper, freshly ground
2 egg whites
3 cups heavy cream
Salted water

Mince boned pike, adding a dash of nutmeg, a few grains of cayenne pepper, and salt and black pepper to taste./ Add egg whites./ Rub mixture through a fine sieve, and place it in a saucepan set on ice./ Beat with a wooden spoon, gradually working in cream./

To form quenelles, use a small scoop and carefully scoop fish mixture into a buttered pan./ Prevent sticking by dipping scoop in warm water./ Pour a little salted water into pan, bring water to a boil, and poach quenelles over low heat for 10 minutes./ Serve with lobster sauce./

Lobster Sauce
1-2 lb. live lobster
1 tbls. butter
1 shallot, chopped
1 cup dry sherry
½ cup heavy cream
1 tsp. salt
Black pepper, freshly ground
2 tbls. cornstarch
¼ cup cold water
Salt

Cut live lobster in 6 or 8 pieces./ In a large saucepan, sauté cut lobster in butter for 3 or 4 minutes./ Add shallot, ½ cup sherry, cream, salt, and pepper to taste, and mix./ Cover the saucepan tightly and simmer for 20 minutes./ Remove lobster from pan./

Cook remaining liquid until it is reduced by one half./ Add cornstarch mixed with cold water, and stir until thickened./ Season with salt and pepper, and add remaining ½ cup of sherry./ Strain through cheesecloth, and serve on quenelles./

Chateau Restaurant

Stuffed Shrimp Parmesan

Serves 6

24 to 30 jumbo shrimp
4 tbls. butter
¾ cup seasoned bread
  crumbs
3 tbls. grated Parmesan
  cheese
Mozzarella cheese, thinly
  sliced and cut into small 1
  by ½ inch pieces

Shell, devein, and clean shrimp. Split each shrimp down the back, being careful not to cut through to the other side./

Melt butter in a saucepan./ Blend bread crumbs and Parmesan cheese with butter to form stuffing./ Mold one teaspoon stuffing onto each shrimp, pressing it firmly by hand./ Place a piece of mozzarella cheese over stuffing./

Place stuffed shrimp on cookie sheet, and bake in a 350° F. oven until cheese is melted./

Charlie W's Restaurant

Baked Fillet Of Sole With Capers

Serves 8

¾ cup butter (or part
  margarine)
Salt
Pepper
8 serving pieces fillet of sole
  (or flounder)
Flour
2 tbls. capers
2 tbls. wine vinegar
1 tsp. anchovy paste (or 4 flat
  anchovies, mashed)
Parsley, chopped
Paprika

Spread ¼ cup butter over bottom of large baking dish./ Lightly salt and pepper fillets and roll them in flour, shaking off excess flour./ Place fillets side by side in baking dish, and dot with remaining butter. In a 350°F. oven, bake the fillets, basting occasionally, 30 to 35 minutes or until fillets seem tender and begin to brown./

Add the capers to the fillets./ Mix vinegar with anchovies, and pour the mixture over the fish, basting well./ Bake fillets 5 to 10 minutes longer./ When sauce is bubbling, remove casserole from oven, sprinkle parsley and paprika over fish, and serve./

Sweet And Sour Fish

Serves 6

6 slices mackerel
2 cups water
2 onions, thinly sliced
2 lemons, sliced
⅓ cup brown sugar
¼ cup seedless raisins
2 tsp. salt
1 bay leaf
6 gingersnaps, crushed
⅓ cup cider vinegar

In a large saucepan, combine mackerel, water, onion, lemon, brown sugar, raisins, salt, and bay leaf./ Cover pot and cook 25 minutes over low heat./ Remove the fish and place on a platter./

Add gingersnaps and vinegar to the fish stock./ Stirring constantly, cook the fish stock over low heat until smooth./ Pour stock over fish on platter./ May be served warm or cold./

Grilled Eel

Serves 6 to 8

2½ lbs. eel
2 tbls. olive oil
Juice of ½ lemon
Salt
Pepper
Marjoram
Grated Parmesan cheese

Skin and cut eel into 2 inch pieces./ Sprinkle pieces with olive oil and lemon juice./ Place the eel on a foil-covered broiler pan and season with salt, pepper and marjoram to taste./

Grill eel in a hot broiler for approximately 15 minutes, or until golden brown./ Sprinkle eel with grated Parmesan cheese and serve./

Eel Dutch Style

Serves 6

2 lbs. eel
Boiling water
⅓ cup onions, sliced
2 sprigs parsley
1 tsp. vinegar
4 whole peppercorns
½ tsp. salt
Lemon slices
¼ cup butter, melted
6 potatoes, boiled

Cut eel into serving pieces./ In a skillet, place eel and add enough boiling water to cover fish, onions, parsley, vinegar, peppercorns and salt./ Bring to a boil, reduce heat and let simmer 10 to 15 minutes, or until eel flakes when tested with a fork./ Place eel on platter and serve with melted butter and boiled potatoes./

Quick Low Calorie Fish Vegetable Bake

Serves 6

1-16 oz. can peas and carrots
1-16 oz. French style green
  beans
2 cans condensed tomato
  soup
½ cup onions, chopped
½ cup green pepper,
  chopped
Garlic powder
Celery seed (or celery salt)
Salt
Potatoes, cubed (optional)
2 pounds of favorite fish
  fillets, e.g. flounder, cod,
  halibut
Paprika

In a large bowl, mix peas and carrots, green beans, tomato soup, onion, green pepper, garlic powder, celery seed, salt to taste, and potatoes, if desired./

Place fish fillets in baking pan./ Spread vegetable mixture over fish, and sprinkle lightly with paprika./ In a 350° F. oven, bake fish 45 minutes to one hour./ Fish vegetable bake may be served warm or cold./

Stuffed Butternut Squash

Serves 4

2 medium butternut squash
4 tbls. water
¼ cup butter
½ lb. mushrooms, sliced
1 pimento, chopped
4 tbls. flour
2 cups light cream
Salt
Pepper
2 cups flaked tuna fish,
  drained
½ cup Gouda or Cheddar
  cheese, grated
2 tbls. bread crumbs
Paprika
Butter

Cut squash in half lengthwise, removing seeds and fibers./ In a baking dish, place squash cut side down./ Add approximately 4 tablespoons water to dish./ Bake squash in a 375° F. oven approximately 30 minutes, or until they are just tender./

Meanwhile, melt butter in a skillet and saute mushrooms and pimento until soft./ Add flour to skillet, and mix well./ Over medium heat, add cream, and cook mixture, stirring constantly, until it thickens./ Season to taste with salt and pepper./ Stir in tuna./

Stuff the tuna mixture into the squash./ Combine cheese and bread crumbs, and sprinkle over tuna./ Sprinkle stuffed squash with paprika and dot with butter./ Return squash to oven, stuffed side up, and bake 15 minutes./

Chef: Nick Domingo   Concord Hotel

Brook Trout With Crabmeat Stuffing

Serves 4

4 whole trout, if frozen
  partially defrost
5 slices white bread
Oil (or butter)
1 small onion, finely diced
½ small green pepper, finely
  diced
1-2 oz. can sliced
  mushrooms, drained
1 can crabmeat, rinsed and
  picked over for shells
2 tbls. mayonnaise
Juice of ½ lemon
1 tbls. parsley, finely
  chopped
Salt
Pepper
Paprika
2 tbls. butter

Rinse trout, pat dry, and set aside./ Grind bread in blender to form crumbs./ In a skillet, sauté onion, green pepper and mushrooms in a small amount of oil or butter until onions are transparent, and add mixture to crumbs in a bowl./ Add crabmeat, mayonnaise, lemon juice, parsley, salt, pepper, and paprika to taste, to bowl./ Mix ingredients well./ Divide mixture and stuff trout with it./

In a buttered pan, place trout and lightly season with salt, pepper paprika and butter./ In a 350° F. oven, bake trout 45 minutes, or until fish flakes easily./

Sauted Shad Roe

Serves 4

2 pairs shad roe
Salt
Black pepper, freshly ground
½ cup flour
1 cup butter
2 tbls. chives, finely cut
1 tbls. parsley, finely
  chopped
2 tsp. lemon juice
1 tsp. Worcestershire sauce
Bacon slices, cooked crisply

With a scissors, slit membranes connecting roe./ Sprinkle roe with salt and pepper to taste./ Flour on both sides, shaking off excess./ In an 8 inch skillet over moderate heat, melt 6 tablespoons butter./ When foam subsides, add roes and sauté for 6 minutes on each side, regulating heat so roes brown quickly and evenly./ When brown, transfer roes to heated platter and keep warm./ Add chives, parsley, lemon juice and Worcestershire sauce to skillet and stir into pan drippings./ Add remaining 2 tablespoons butter and mix sauce together thoroughly./ Pour sauce over roes./ Serve at once topped with bacon slices./

Century Hotel

Gefilte Fish

Yield: 10 to 12 pieces

3½ lbs. whitefish and yellow
  pike, in equal parts, filleted
  and ground
½ cup + 1 heaping tbls.
  matzo meal
½ cup water
2 eggs
1 medium onion, grated
7 tsp. salt
2 tsp. sugar
1 tsp. white pepper
4 cups water
Heads, skin, and bones of
  fish
2 large carrots, sliced
2 large onions, thinly sliced

Mix fish, matzo meal, ½ cup water, eggs, onion, 4 teaspoons salt, one teaspoon sugar and ½ teaspoon white pepper until mixture becomes pasty./

In a large pot with tightly fitting cover, combine 4 cups water with fish heads, skin, and bones, carrots and onions./ Bring stock to boil and simmer for 5 minutes./ Add one tablespoon salt, 1 tsp. sugar, and ½ teaspoon pepper to stock, and simmer 5 minutes longer./

With moistened hands, shape fish mixture into oval shaped patties./ Carefully drop each patty into boiling broth./ Cover pot and lower heat; simmer slowly for 1¼ hours, without uncovering./ Adjust seasoning to taste./ Cook ¾ hour longer./

Cool patties in broth ½ hour./ Remove fish patties to fish platter and place carrot slices on top./ Strain broth over fish, and chill./ Serve fish with horseradish on the side./

Stuffed Sole

Serves 4

2 lbs. fillets of sole
2 tbls. lemon juice
1 clove garlic, crushed
Herbs
1 cup mushrooms, sliced
¼ cup onions, diced
¼ cup celery, diced
2 tbls. butter
2 cups whole wheat bread,
  crumbled
½ tsp. sage
Seasonings
1 cup bouillon (or soup stock
  or water)

Choose fillets of sole that are small, white, and firm./ Brush fillets with mixture of lemon juice, garlic, and herbs of your choice./

To prepare stuffing, in a skillet sauté mushrooms, onion, and celery in butter./ Add crumbled bread, sage, and seasonings to taste, and enough bouillon to bind the mixture together./

Spread stuffing in the bottom of a shallow baking dish./ Arrange fillets on top of stuffing and bake in a 350° F. oven for 30 minutes./

The stuffing can also be used in baking other whole fish./

White Fish Casserole

Serves 4

1 large onion, quartered and
  sliced
2 tbls. oil (or margarine)
4 carrots, quartered and
  sliced
1 rib celery, finely sliced
1 tsp. sugar
½ cup water
4 or 5 slices white fish
Margarine
Fresh parsley, chopped
4 potatoes, sliced

In a casserole, sauté onion in oil until onion is soft and transparent./ Add carrots and celery to the casserole and sprinkle sugar on top./ Add approximately ¼ cup water, cover the casserole, and steam it over low heat for about 5 minutes./

Add white fish to casserole, and top fish with margarine and parsley./ Arrange potato slices over fish, adding margarine and sprinkling with parsley./ Add ¼ cup water, more if necessary, and steam cook the casserole for 40 minutes./

Serve fish with carrot sauce and potatoes on the side./

Trout In White Wine

Serves 1

1 trout
Salt
Pepper
Juice of one lemon
½ cup white wine (or
  champagne)
½ cup heavy cream

Season trout with salt and pepper to taste./ Place trout in a buttered casserole, and sprinkle with the lemon juice./ Pour wine over trout, cover casserole and bake in 350° F. oven for 15 minutes./

Pour cream over fish, and place open casserole under broiler until sauce is brown./ Keep broiler door open and watch carefully./ Serve trout hot./

Eldred Fish Preserve

Baked Stuffed Shad

Serves 4

2 large onions, sliced
4 tbls. butter
1 cup bread crumbs
¼ cup parsley, finely
  chopped
1 egg, well beaten
2 tbls. celery leaves, finely
  chopped
1 tsp. salt
½ tsp. dried thyme
1 split and boned shad

In a skillet, sauté onions in butter until soft./ Add remaining ingredients except fish and mix well./ Stuff shad with mixture and sew up or secure with string./ Place stuffed shad in a greased baking dish./ In a 400° F. oven, bake for 30 to 40 minutes./

Tempura

Serves 4

Batter
½ cup flour
6½ tbls. water
1 egg, beaten
½ tsp. baking soda

In a bowl, lightly and quickly mix all ingredients together./ Batter need not be completely smooth./

Preparation
Cooking oil or shortening
Filet of sole, cut into bite-
  size pieces
Shrimp
Carrot strips
Green pepper strips
Onion rings
Green beans
Salt
Lemon wedges

Fill a deep fryer or deep skillet approximately one third full of cooking oil./ Heat fat to 365° F./ If using a deep fryer, lower basket into hot fat./ Dip fish, shrimp or vegetable pieces, a few at a time, into batter and drop into hot fat./ Fry for 2 minutes or until golden./ Drain on absorbent paper, sprinkle with salt./ Serve hot with lemon wedges and soy sauce or with Tempura or "plum" sauce./

Tempura Sauce
1 cup beef bouillon or broth
¾ cup soy sauce
¼ cup saki
¼ cup sherry or saki
4 tbls. sugar

Mix all ingredients together and serve in small individual dipping bowls./

Sweet-Sour "Plum" Sauce
2 tbls. chili sauce
2 tbls. black raspberry
  preserves
5 dashes Tabasco
½ tsp. dry mustard

Combine all ingredients and mix together well./

Baked Herring

Serves 2

1 large pickling herring
2 onions, sliced
Butter
Matzo meal
Paprika
Sweet cream

Skin and filet herring and soak in water to cover overnight./ In an ovenproof pan, sauté onions in butter./ Roll herring in matzo meal with a pinch of paprika and lay in pan with onions./ Cover fish with sweet cream./ In a 375° F. oven, bake for 35 minutes./

Marinated Carp

Serves 6

6 slices carp
4 onions, sliced
2 cups water
1½ tsp. salt
¼ tsp. pepper
½ cup white vinegar
1½ tbls. sugar
2 bay leaves
2 tsp. pickling spices

In a saucepan, combine carp, 2 sliced onions, water, salt and pepper./ Bring to a boil, reduce heat and cook for 25 minutes./ Carefully remove fish and place in a bowl or jar alternating in layers with remaining 2 sliced onions./ Combine vinegar, sugar, bay leaves and pickling spices and add to fish stock./ Bring to a boil, pour over carp, cover and let pickle in refrigerator for 2 days before serving./ Marinated carp will keep for 2 weeks./

Grossinger Hotel

Ultimate Trout

Serves 6

6 fresh trout
2 cups milk
2 large lemons
¼ cup capers
½ cup flour
Salt
Freshly ground black pepper
4 tbls. butter
Vegetable oil

Clean and rinse trout inside and out under cold running water./ Place trout in shallow pan, cover with cold milk and let stand one half hour./

Peel and section lemons, removing all white pulp, seeds and membranes./ Cut into small cubes, mix with capers and set aside./

Drain but do not dry fish./ Coat it with flour seasoned with salt and pepper./ In large skillet, brown trout in ¼ inch oil until golden./ Turn and repeat./ Transfer fish to heated platter, drain oil from skillet and wipe clean./ Add butter to skillet and slowly let it brown./ Scatter lemon cubes and capers over trout./ Pour browned butter over and serve./

The Turner Brook Reserve

Meats

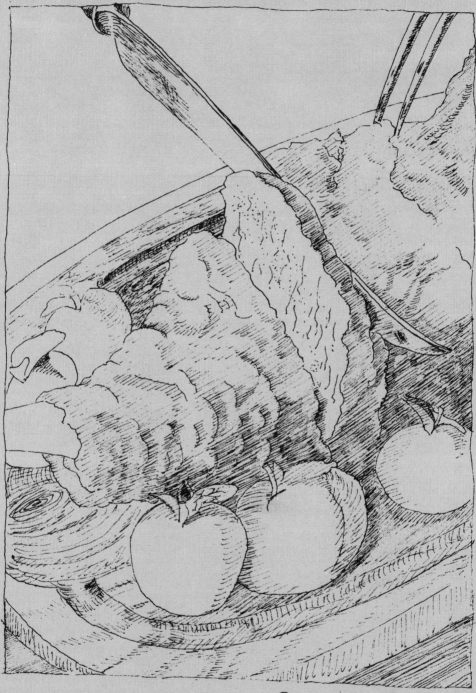

Bud Wertheim '75

Pepper Steak With Onions

Serves 4

4 green peppers, seeded and
   cut into large squares
1 tsp. baking soda
Water
6 tbls. peanut oil
1 lb. steak, cut in narrow
   strips
4 tbls. cornstarch
1 large onion, sliced
4 tbls. sherry wine
2½ cups beef broth (or
   water)
1 tsp. monosodium glutamate
1 tsp. sugar
1 tsp. salt
4 tbls. soy sauce

Place peppers in a pot of boiling water with baking soda for 3 minutes./ Drain peppers, and rinse in cold water./

In a heavy skillet, heat 4 tablespoons oil./ Sprinkle 2 tablespoons cornstarch and 2 tablespoons oil on meat./ Place meat, onion, and peppers in pan, and brown quickly, stirring mixture a few times./

Add sherry wine, cover pan, and cook for approximately one minute./ Add broth, replace cover, and cook over low heat for 5 minutes./ Remove cover and add Accent, sugar, salt, and 2 tablespoons cornstarch mixed with soy sauce to pan./ Stir mixture with wooden spoon until it comes to boil; then cook for 2 minutes more./ Serve pepper steak with rice./

Canton Restaurant

Roast Leg Of Lamb

Serves 6 to 8

6 to 7 lb. leg of lamb
Salt
Pepper
½ tsp. marjoram
¼ tsp. oregano
3 to 4 large cloves garlic,
   mashed
2 tsp. Dijon mustard
1 tsp. paprika
3 tbls. olive oil
1 onion, finely minced
1 carrot, finely minced
1 stalk celery, finely minced
Flour
2 to 3 cups warm lamb stock
   or beef broth
1 tbls. flour
1 tbls. butter

Dry lamb thoroughly with paper towels./ Season with salt and pepper to taste, marjoram and oregano./ Make slits in meaty part of leg and insert small bits of garlic./ In a small bowl, combine mustard and paprika, then rub mixture over lamb./ Let lamb stand at room temperature for 30 minutes to one hour./

In a large baking dish or roasting pan, heat oil, add minced onion, carrot and celery, and cook mixture without browning for 2 to 3 minutes./ Sprinkle lamb lightly with flour and place in baking dish./ In a 375° F. oven, roast for one hour and 30 minutes, basting every 30 minutes with warm stock./ When done, remove to serving platter and let rest for 20 minutes before carving./

Add any remaining stock to baking dish, scrape loose brown particles, and bring to a boil over high heat./ Strain pan juices into small saucepan./ Combine flour and butter and roll between hands into a ball./ Cook pan juices over high heat, gradually whisking in small bits of flour-butter ball until sauce is thickened./ Season with salt and pepper to taste./ Serve lamb with sauce on the side./

Osso Buco

Serves 12

7 lbs. veal shins, sawed into
12-2½ inch pieces
1 cup flour
1 cup peanut oil
4 tbls. butter
½ cup onions, chopped
finely
½ cup sherry wine
4 cups beef consommé
½ cup mushrooms, chopped
finely
½ cup carrots, chopped
finely
½ cup prosciutto ham, cut in
small pieces
Salt
Parsley flakes
Black pepper

Be sure the veal bones are well covered with meat./ Roll each piece lightly in flour./ In a large, heavy pan, warm oil./ Place veal pieces side by side, and let them cook over very low heat for 10 minutes./ Turn and cook 10 additional minutes./ Remove from pan, and drain oil from veal./

Scrape remaining oil from pan./ Melt butter in pan, add onions, and brown them./ Add sherry and simmer mixture a few minutes./ Add consommé, mushrooms, carrot, ham, salt to taste, and pinches of parsley and pepper, and blend well./

Return meat to pan, cover and cook over very low heat approximately 25 minutes, or until meat is tender when pierced with fork./ Serve over risotto or boiled rice./

D'z Restaurant

Roulade of Beef

Serves 8

2½ lbs. top round of beef,
cut into 8 slices ap-
proximately 2½ by 4 inches
Salt
Pepper
Paprika
Prepared mustard
8 tsp. onion, finely chopped
2 eggs, hard-boiled and cut
in quarters
2 frankfurters, cut in quarters
lengthwise
8 small slices bacon
8 small slices sour pickle
Flour
6 tbls. butter
4 large onions, cut in cubes

Place beef slices on a board, cover with wax paper and pound with the bottom of a small iron skillet until slice is approximately ¼ inch thick./ Season with salt and pepper to taste, dash of paprika, and a little mustard applied with the tip of a knife./

On each slice of beef, sprinkle one teaspoon onion, and place ¼ hard boiled egg, ¼ frankfurter, slice of bacon, and slice of pickle./ Roll the beef, tie or skewer it with toothpicks and roll in flour./

In a skillet, heat 4 tablespoons butter, and sauté onion cubes until they are transparent and very lightly browned./ Remove onions from skillet, and spread them in large covered baking pan./ Cover pan and place in a preheated 375° F. oven./

Add 2 tablespoons butter to same skillet and brown roulades./ As roulades brown, place them on top of onions in oven./ Cover pan and bake for 1½ hours./ Serve roulades with rice./

Slavia Mt. Resort

Hungarian Goulash

Serves 4 to 6

2 tbls. oil
2 onions, sliced thinly
2 lbs. middle chuck meat,
  cut into cubes
1 green pepper, sliced in
  strips
2 tbls. tomato paste
2 tsp. sweet Hungarian
  paprika
1 tsp. salt
1 tsp. caraway seeds
1 tsp. marjoram
2 tsp. cider vinegar
2 cups chicken broth

In a heavy saucepan cook onions in oil until they are transparent./ Remove onions, add meat to saucepan, and brown cubes./ Return onions to pan and add green pepper, tomato paste, paprika, salt, caraway seeds, and marjoram./ Stir mixture with wooden spoon./ Add vinegar and chicken broth and bring to boil./ Cover saucepan and cook over low heat approximately 1½ hours, or until meat is tender./ Serve with boiled potatoes or noodles./

Piquant Meat Balls

Serves 6 to 8

2 lbs. chopped meat
1 medium onion, grated
2 eggs, lightly beaten
2 slices white bread, soaked
  in ¼ cup water or milk
1 heaping tbls. dark brown
  sugar
1 tsp. lemon juice
Salt
Pepper
2 large onions, chopped
10 dried apricots
½ cup water
2 cups boiling water
Juice of one lemon
½ cup dark brown sugar
½ cup seedless raisins
6 tbls. catsup

Mix meat, grated onion, eggs, bread, brown sugar, lemon juice, and salt and pepper to taste and shape into balls./ Place meatballs on greased cookie sheet with sides and bake in a 500° F. oven until lightly brown./

To make sauce, cook chopped onion and apricots in ½ cup water until soft./ Strain or blend mixture, and add boiling water, lemon juice, brown sugar, raisins and catsup./ Cook sauce in pot, uncovered, for ½ hour./ Add meatballs to pot and cook an additional ½ hour./ Add salt and pepper to taste./

Spareribs With Sauerkraut, Polish Style

Serves 4 to 6

2 tbls. vegetable oil
3 lbs. spareribs, cut into
  individual pieces
1½ cups onions, coarsely
  chopped
2 cloves garlic, minced
2 cups boiling water
1 bay leaf
1½ tsp. salt
½ tsp. pepper, freshly
  ground
1 lb. sauerkraut
1 apple, peeled, cored and
  chopped
½ cup fine barley
1 tsp. caraway seeds

In a Dutch oven or large saucepan, heat oil and brown ribs over high heat./ Add onions and garlic, reduce heat to low, and cook for 10 minutes./ Mix in one cup boiling water, bay leaf, salt and pepper and cook 30 minutes, stirring occasionally./ Add remaining one cup water, undrained sauerkraut, apple, barley, and caraway seeds./ Mix well and continue cooking one hour longer./ Correct seasoning and discard bay leaf before serving./

Shredded Beef Szechewan Style

Serves 4

2 tbls. peanut oil
Flank steak (or other tender
  beef), shredded
½ cup + 1 tsp. soy sauce
2 tbls. + 1 tsp. cornstarch
3 stalks celery, shredded
1 green pepper, seeded and
  shredded
1 carrot, peeled and
  shredded
½ cup bamboo shoots,
  shredded
1 tsp. crushed red pepper
1 clove garlic, crushed
1 slice ginger, chopped
¼ tsp. sugar
¼ tsp. black pepper
1 tbls. dry sherry
½ cup cold water

In a wok or large fry pan, heat one tablespoon oil over high heat./ Mix shredded beef with one teaspoon soy sauce and one teaspoon cornstarch, and add to wok, mixing thoroughly for 2 minutes./ Remove from wok and set aside./

In a clean pan, heat one tablespoon oil, add celery and green pepper, and sauté for one minute./ Add carrot and bamboo shoots to pan, mix with other vegetables, and sauté one additional minute./ Add vegetables to the meat./

In a clean pan over high heat, sauté red pepper, garlic and ginger./ Add meat and vegetables./ Add ½ cup soy sauce, sugar, black pepper, and sherry and mix well./ When mixture begins to boil, thicken it with 2 tablespoons cornstarch mixed with cold water./

Chef: Ching Wah Nieh   *Concord Hotel*

Flank Steak

Serves 8

1 large flank steak
Salt
Pepper
Flour
3 tbls. butter
2 large Bermuda onions,
  peeled, quartered, and
  sliced
1-32 oz. can stewed tomatoes

Sprinkle steak on both sides with salt and pepper to taste, and flour./ Place steak in a shallow roasting pan, and dot with butter./ In a preheated 550° F. oven, bake steak approximately 5 minutes./ When sizzling, turn meat and bake 5 additional minutes./

Add onions to pan; allow them to soften and brown in pan juices, then pile them on top of steak./ Drain tomatoes, reserving juice, and spread over onions./ Reduce heat to 325° F. and bake steak one hour, basting occasionally with pan juices and juice from tomatoes./ Repile vegetables on meat when they slip off./ After one hour, reduce heat further; meat can be kept warm almost indefinitely./

Macaroni And Beef Casserole

Serves 10 to 12

1 lb. or more beef shank
½ tsp. thyme
2 onions, chopped
1 tbls. margarine
1-32 oz. can tomato purée
1-32 oz. can tomato juice
1-16 oz. can stewed
  tomatoes
Salt
Water
1 tsp. oregano
1 quart shell macaroni,
  uncooked
Buttered crumbs or grated
  cheese (optional)

In a roasting pan, bake beef shank with thyme in a 300° F. oven for 2 hours, or until beef is tender./

In a large pot, sauté chopped onions in margarine until they are transparent./ Add tomato purée, tomato juice, and stewed tomatoes, oregano, and 2 teaspoons salt to onions./ Simmer mixture 2 hours./ Adjust seasoning to taste./

Boil shell macaroni in water with one teaspoon salt until tender./ Drain macaroni./

Cut meat from shank bone and remove fat./ Grind meat and add to tomato sauce./ Add macaroni to mixture./ Stir macaroni, meat, and sauce briefly, and ladle into one large or several individual casseroles./ Top with buttered crumbs or grated cheese, if desired./ Heat casseroles in oven until serving time./

(Beef shank, fat, and trimmings may be boiled with salt, one teaspoon vinegar, water, and one chopped onion to make beef broth./ Skim when cool for clear broth, or add to warmed-over macaroni and beef casserole to moisten.)/

Baked Pork Chops

Serves 6

6 pork chops, about ¾" thick
Salt
Pepper
2 carrots, thinly sliced
6 green onions, finely
  chopped
Paprika
4 tbls. sour cream
1-20 oz. can creamed corn
¼ cup corn flakes, finely
  crushed
Butter or margarine

In a skillet, brown chops./ Season with salt and pepper to taste./ In the bottom of a large casserole, place a layer of carrots, and top with browned chops./ Cover chops with onions and sprinkle generously with paprika./ Combine sour cream and corn and add to casserole./ Season with salt and pepper once more./ Top with corn flakes and dot with butter./ Cover casserole and bake in a 350° F. oven for 45 minutes or until chops are tender./

Pizza Meat Loaf

Serves 6 to 8

1 egg
1½ cups (or a 10½ oz. can)
  pizza sauce
3 cups corn flakes
1½ tsp. salt
¼ tsp. pepper
2 lbs. ground beef
¼ cup onion, finely chopped
⅔ cup (or 1-4 oz. can)
  mushrooms, sliced
  (optional)
6 oz. mozzarella cheese,
  sliced

In a large mixing bowl, combine egg, pizza sauce, corn flakes, salt and pepper./ Add beef, onions (and mushrooms, if desired), mixing lightly but thoroughly./ In the bottom of an ungreased 8 by 8 by 2 inch baking pan, press half the meat mixture evenly./ Place several slices of cheese on top./ Spread remaining meat mixture evenly over cheese./ In a 350° F. oven, bake approximately one hour, or until meat begins to shrink from sides of pan./

Cut remaining cheese into narrow strips and lattice them diagonally over top of meat loaf./ Bake 3 minutes longer or until cheese strips are slightly melted./ Cut meat loaf into squares; serve hot./

Onion And Beefburgers

Serves 6 to 8

1½ lbs. ground beef
4 tbls. onion, grated
2 cloves garlic, minced
1 egg
¼ cup potato, grated and
  drained
¼ cup water
2 tsp. salt
¼ tsp. pepper
3 tbls. fat
2 onions, sliced

In a large bowl, combine beef, grated onion, garlic, egg, potato, water, salt, and pepper, and mix well./ Form mixture into 8 hamburger patties./

In a skillet, melt the fat and add the hamburgers and sliced onions./ Brown meat 10 minutes on one side; then turn and fry for another 5 minutes./

Potted Steak Esterhazy, Hungarian

Serves 6

*2 lbs. round steak, cut into 6
 portions*
Oil
*3 carrots, cut into strips ½ by
 ¼ inch thick*
*2 medium onions, thinly
 sliced*
*3 stalks celery, cut into strips
 ½ by ¼ inch thick*
½ cup white sauterne wine
*2 cups brown gravy,
 packaged or canned*
1 cup beef stock
½ cup tomato puree
2 tsp. dry mustard
*¼ tsp. pepper, freshly
 ground*

In a skillet, heat oil and sauté steak until it is lightly browned on both sides./ Remove steak./ In same skillet, sauté carrots, onion and celery until lightly browned./ Add wine and continue cooking until liquid is reduced by half./ Add gravy, beef stock, tomato purée, mustard, and pepper./ Mix well./ Simmer sauce 5 minutes./

Place steaks in square pan and cover with sauce./ In a 350° F. oven, cook steak for one hour 25 minutes./

Chef: Mr. Hazy   *Olympic Hotel*

Holubtsi (Stuffed Cabbage)

Yield: approximately 20 rolls

1 head cabbage (about 3 lbs.)
Boiling water
½ cup rice
2 tbls. fat
1 onion, chopped
*1 lb. ground beef (can be
 mixed with pork)*
2 tsp. salt
½ tsp. pepper
1-8 oz. can tomato sauce
Bacon slices

In a deep pot, pour enough boiling water to cover over cabbage, cover pot, and let soak 15 minutes./ Drain and remove leaves carefully from head, shaving off thick part without cutting through./

In a saucepan, bring one cup of water to a boil, add rice and cook 10 minutes./ Drain and reserve./ Heat fat in a frying pan and lightly brown onion in it./ Combine onion with rice, ground meat, one teaspoon salt and ¼ teaspoon pepper./ Place some of meat mixture in a cabbage leaf, turn in sides and roll up carefully./ Repeat process until all stuffing is used and several cabbage leaves remain./

In a saucepan, boil tomato sauce with one cup of water, one teaspoon salt and ¼ teaspoon pepper./ Line bottom of baking pan with remaining cabbage leaves and top with cabbage rolls./ Pour tomato sauce over./ Cover with bacon slices./ In a 375° F. oven bake for 1½ hours./

Glen Spa Restaurant

Stuffed Peppers

Serves 4

4 green peppers
1 cup tomato sauce
1 egg, beaten
1 tsp. salt
¼ tsp. oregano
Pepper
1 lb. ground round steak
2 onions
2 tbls. uncooked rice
1 tbls. dried parsley
½ cup boiling water

Wash peppers, cut a one inch piece from the stem end and reserve./ Clean peppers, scooping out seeds and fibers carefully./ Mix together one half of the tomato sauce, egg, salt, oregano and a pinch of pepper./ Add meat, one minced onion, rice and parsley and mix well./ Stuff peppers lightly with mixture./

Slice the remaining onion and place it in the bottom of a baking dish./ Arrange stuffed peppers on top./ Replace reserved pepper ends./ Combine remaining tomato sauce with boiling water and pour over peppers./ In a 325° F. oven, bake, uncovered, for 1½ hours./ During baking, baste several times with pan liquids./

Ted's Restaurant

Stuffed Flank Steak

Serves 6

½ lb. bulk pork sausage
1 cup soft bread crumbs
½ cup onions, chopped
1 tbls. parsley, minced
1 tsp. sage
¼ tsp. baking powder
2 eggs, lightly beaten
1 large flank steak
Salt
Pepper
2 tbls. shortening
1 cup catsup

To make stuffing, combine pork sausage, bread crumbs, onions, parsley, sage, and baking powder./ Moisten mixture with eggs./

Score steak with knife on both sides, and sprinkle meat with salt and pepper to taste./ Spoon stuffing on steak./ Beginning at narrow end, roll up steak and sew edges together or skewer edges with thin metal skewer./ In a skillet, heat shortening and brown stuffed meat./

In a 3 quart casserole, place stuffed meat sewn side down and spread with catsup./ In a preheated 350° F. oven, bake meat in covered casserole for one hour./ Uncover casserole and bake meat for 30 additional minutes or until tender./

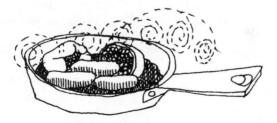

Lamb And Beans Provençale

Serves 6 to 8

1 lb. dried navy beans (or pea
  beans or 2-1 lb. cans of
  Great Northern beans,
  drained)
Water
¼ cup oil
2 lbs. onions, thinly sliced
2 cloves garlic, crushed
2 lbs. shoulder of lamb,
  cubed
1 large can Italian plum
  tomatoes
1 tsp. salt
½ tsp. pepper
½ tsp. rosemary
½ tsp. marjoram

In a 6 quart kettle, combine beans with 6 cups of water./ Bring mixture to a boil, simmer for 5 minutes, then remove kettle from heat and cover it./ Let kettle stand one hour./ Drain beans, reserving liquid./ Add water to liquid to measure 2 quarts./ Return beans and liquid to kettle, and boil slowly for one hour or until beans are tender./ Drain beans./

In a large flame-proof casserole, heat oil and sauté onions and garlic until they are golden./ Add lamb cubes to the casserole, and cook until cubes are coated with oil./ Add tomatoes, salt and pepper (adjust measurements to taste), rosemary, and marjoram./ Cover casserole and cook in a 350° F. oven, stirring occasionally, for 2 to 3 hours, until lamb is very tender./

Lamb Shank Stew

Serves 4 to 6

4 lbs. lamb shanks
¼ cup oil
2 lbs. small potatoes (or large
  potatoes, cut) peeled
1 lb. small white onions
2 cups canned tomatoes
1-6 oz. can tomato paste
¾ cup dry red wine
2 tbls. wine vinegar
1 to 2 cloves garlic
2 tsp. salt
1 or 2 bay leaves
1 strip lemon peel

In Dutch oven or casserole, brown meat in heated oil./ Remove meat./ Brown potatoes and onions in remaining fat./ Return meat to casserole./

Combine tomatoes, tomato paste, wine vinegar, garlic, and salt./ Blend in electric blender until smooth./ Pour mixture over meat and vegetables in casserole./ Add bay leaves and lemon peel./ Cover and simmer casserole until meat is tender, about 1½ hours./

Veal Cutlets Parmigiana

Serves 4

1 lb. veal cutlets
¼ cup flour
2 eggs
Salt
Pepper
1 cup bread crumbs
3 tbls. grated Parmesan
  cheese
6 tbls. olive oil
1½ cups tomato sauce
½ lb. mozzarella cheese

Coat veal cutlets lightly with flour, dip in eggs beaten with salt and pepper to taste, then in mixture of bread crumbs and Parmesan cheese, coating both sides heavily./ In a skillet, fry cutlets in hot oil until golden brown./

In baking dish, arrange veal and pour tomato sauce over the cutlets./ Slice cheese thinly and place over each cutlet./ Bake veal in a 350° F. oven for 15 minutes./

The Lighthouse Restaurant

Moussaka

Serves 8 to 10

3 medium eggplants, peeled
    and cut in ½ inch slices
1 cup butter
3 large onions, finely
    chopped
2 lbs. ground lamb or beef or
    a combination of both
½ cup red wine
½ cup parsley, chopped
3 tbls. tomato paste
¼ tsp. allspice
Salt
Pepper
6 tbls. flour
1 quart milk
2 cups ricotta or cottage
    cheese
4 eggs, beaten
Nutmeg
1 cup bread crumbs
1 cup Parmesan cheese

In a large frying pan, brown eggplant slices quickly in 4 tablespoons of butter./ Remove eggplant and set aside./ Add 4 more tablespoons of butter to pan and brown onions./ Add meat and cook 10 minutes more./ Combine wine, parsley, tomato paste, allspice and salt and pepper to taste and stir into meat./ Simmer mixture until all liquid is absorbed./

Meanwhile, in a large saucepan, melt 8 tablespoons butter, then blend in flour./ Bring milk to a boil and add it gradually, stirring constantly, until mixture is thickened and smooth./ Remove from heat, cool slightly, and stir in ricotta cheese, eggs and nutmeg to taste./

Grease an 11 by 16 inch baking pan./ Sprinkle bottom with layer of bread crumbs./ Make layers alternating eggplant and meat sauce and sprinkle each layer with bread crumbs and Parmesan cheese./ Pour cheese sauce over all./ In a 375° F. oven, bake moussaka for one hour or until top is golden./ Remove from oven and allow to cool for 20 to 30 minutes before serving./ To serve, cut into squares./ (Flavor improves when prepared a day in advance of serving and reheated.)/

Beef Stroganov

Serves 6

2 lbs. lean steak
2 tbls. vegetable oil
3 cloves garlic, crushed
1 onion, minced
1 bay leaf
½ tsp. caraway seeds
3 tbls. Hungarian paprika
1 quart water
1 tbls. salt
¼ tsp. white pepper
¼ tsp. Worcestershire sauce
2 cups flour
2 tbls. cornstarch
1 quart liquid non-dairy
    cream
2 tbls. Burgundy wine

Cut meat into narrow strips 2 inches by ½ inch thick./ In a heavy pot, heat the oil, then add the meat, garlic, and onion./ Brown the meat quickly on both sides./ Add bay leaf, caraway seeds, 2 tablespoons paprika, water, salt, pepper, and Worcestershire sauce./ Simmer ingredients until meat is nearly soft./

Mix flour, one tablespoon paprika, and cornstarch and stir into liquid non-dairy cream./ Add some hot sauce from the pot to the liquid non-dairy cream mixture, then pour it back slowly, stirring, onto simmering beef./ Add wine and cook until meat is tender./

Chef: Stanley Blum   *Homowack Lodge*

Hungarian Veal Stew

Serves 4

2 tbls. oil
1 onion, diced
*2 tbls. chicken bouillon
   powder*
*1 tbls. Hungarian sweet
   paprika*
2 lbs. lean veal, cubed
Hot water
Veal bone
Flour
Cold water
*1 cup sour cream, at room
   temperature*
Salt

In a heavy saucepan, heat oil and sauté onion until it is transparent./ Remove pan from heat, add chicken bouillon and paprika and mix well./ Return pan to heat, and add veal cubes./ Cook until meat loses its redness./

Cover meat with hot water and simmer for 45 to 60 minutes./ (A veal bone may be added while cooking to enhance the gravy's flavor.)/ Thicken gravy with flour mixed with cold water./ Stir in sour cream./ Season with salt to taste./ Serve stew over broad noodles or dumplings./

Shish Kebab

Serves 6 to 8

*1 boned leg of lamb, with
   most of fat and gristle
   removed*
4 medium onions, chopped
Juice of 1 lemon
¼ cup olive oil
1 tsp. sweet basil (or mint)
Salt
Pepper, freshly ground
Tomatoes, broiled
Green peppers, broiled
Small onions, broiled

Cut lamb into 1½ inch squares./ Mix squares with onions, lemon juice, oil, and basil./ Marinate mixture overnight, or at least a few hours./ Season meat with salt and pepper to taste./

Put the marinated meat on skewers, and broil over charcoal or under broiler./ Keep turning skewers until meat is browned all over./ Serve with broiled tomatoes, green peppers, and small onions./ (Shish kebab may also be prepared by alternating tomatoes, peppers, and small onions on skewers with meat, instead of broiling vegetables separately.)/

Serve shish kebab with rice pilaf, using 4 to 6 cubes of meat per person./

Candied Corned Beef

Serves 8 to 10

*1-5 to 6 lb. first-cut corned
   beef*
Water
*2-8 oz. cans crushed
   pineapple*
¾ cup yellow mustard
½ cup light brown sugar
2 jars spiced peaches
6 whole cloves

Place the corned beef in a Dutch oven./ Barely cover corned beef with cold water./ Bring water to a boil, and drain beef./ Add fresh boiling water to barely cover beef./ Bring to a boil, and cover Dutch oven tightly./ Reduce heat, and simmer gently 2½ to 3 hours or until beef is tender when pricked with a fork./ Remove the beef and cut off any surface fat./

Mix pineapple, mustard, and brown sugar well./ Place corned beef in a roasting pan, and spread pineapple mixture over top and sides of beef./ Add peaches with juice and cloves to pan./ Bake in a preheated 350° F. oven for one hour./

Muriel's Favorite Stuffed Cabbage

Yield: 48 rolls

1 large or 2 medium heads of
   cabbage, preferably Savoy
Boiling water
3 lbs. lean ground beef
2 large Bermuda onions
1 cup quick-cooking oatmeal
2 large eggs
4 tsp. salt
1 garlic clove, minced
½ tsp. white pepper
1-28 oz. can tomato juice
2 dozen dried apricot halves,
   cut into small pieces
1 cup golden raisins
3 tbls. brown sugar
1 to 1½ tsp. sour salt
1-28 oz. can tomato purée
1-8 oz. can tomato sauce
Juice of one lemon
2 tbls. raspberry preserves

Core cabbage, invert in a large covered pot with boiling water to cover, and steam, simmering for 5 minutes./ Drain and remove leaves carefully, cutting any hard core from individual leaves./ Cut very large leaves in half, and pair up smaller ones for stuffing./

Mix the ground beef with one chopped onion, oatmeal, eggs, 2 teaspoons salt, garlic, ¼ teaspoon pepper and enough tomato juice to make a soft, moist mixture./ Place a small ball of stuffing on each cabbage leaf or pair and roll, tucking in side ends securely after the first roll./

Dice remaining onion and spread on bottom of a deep roasting pan./ Add to the pan, apricots, raisins, brown sugar, sour salt, 2 teaspoons salt, ¼ teaspoon pepper and any leftover cabbage which has been diced./ Pour 1¾ cups tomato purée, ½ cup tomato sauce and the balance of the tomato juice over mixture./ Place cabbage rolls close together on top./ Pour the balance of the tomato purée and tomato sauce over cabbage./ Add enough boiling water to barely cover cabbage rolls./ In a 325°F. oven, bake uncovered for approximately 1½ hours./ (If sauce gets too thick, add a little boiling water; if rolls start to brown too much, cover pan with aluminum foil.)/ Mix lemon juice with raspberry preserves and add to sauce./ Shake pan gently to stir./ Continue baking for 15 minutes more./ Correct seasoning./ Stuffed cabbage tastes best if prepared a day in advance of serving./

Veal And Peppers

Serves 4

1 lb. veal scallops
4 tbls. olive oil
1-20 oz. can tomatoes
1½ tsp. salt
¼ tsp. pepper, freshly
   ground
4 large, firm green peppers,
   cleaned, seeded and cut
   into strips
1 large onion, sliced
½ cup dry white wine

Slice veal into thin strips./ In a skillet, heat 2 tablespoons of oil and brown veal on all sides./ Add tomatoes, salt and pepper, cover and simmer over low heat for approximately 20 minutes./ Meanwhile, in another skillet, fry peppers and onion in remaining oil until tender, approximately 15 minutes./ Mix with veal./ Add wine to skillet and reduce over medium heat for 3 minutes./ Lower heat, cover, and simmer over low heat for 15 minutes more./

Chef: John Calderon   *Hotel Gibber*

Beef Hash

Serves 4

2 cups potato purée
3 tbls. butter
Oil
2 large onions, finely
  chopped
2 tomatoes, peeled, seeded,
  and diced
3 cups leftover boiled
  (braised or roast) beef,
  minced
Salt
Pepper
½ cup Gruyère cheese,
  grated

Butter a shallow oven dish, and spread half the potato puree in it./
In a skillet, sauté the chopped onions in a small amount of oil./ When onions are pale yellow, add the tomatoes./ Cook for 3 minutes and then add minced beef./ Season with salt and pepper to taste, and mix well./ Cook ingredients 3 additional minutes./
Spread the beef mixture over potatoes in the dish, and cover it with the rest of the potatoes./ Sprinkle with grated cheese, and brown hash in a 400° F. oven./

Chili Con Carne

Serves 6

3 tbls. vegetable oil
2 cloves garlic, finely
  chopped
1 cup onion, thinly sliced
1 lb. ground round steak
3 tbls. chili powder (or more,
  to taste)
2 cups canned Italian plum
  tomatoes
1½ cups beef broth (or
  water)
1 tsp. salt
Oregano
4 cups canned red kidney
  beans

In a large skillet, heat oil, add garlic and onion, and cook until lightly browned./ Add meat to skillet and cook, stirring with wooden spoon, until meat loses its red color./ Stir in chili powder./ Add tomatoes, beef broth, salt, and a pinch of oregano to skillet./ Reduce heat, cover and simmer mixture for one hour./ Add beans to mixture and cook an additional half hour./ Serve chile con carne with old fashioned soda crackers./

(As variations, add ⅛ cup green pepper cut into strips when browning garlic and onion; or add one tablespoon pine nuts and ¼ cup black olives, pitted and cut into small pieces, when ready to serve.)/

Fresh Kolbasi

Yield: 10 lbs.

5 lbs. boneless pork
5 lbs. hamburger meat
1 tbls. salt
1 tsp. black pepper
2 cloves garlic, crushed and
  minced
Beef or pork casings

Cut pork into ¼ inch pieces, including fat and lean pieces, and place in bowl./ Add hamburger to pork, and season with salt, pepper, and garlic./ Mix ingredients well./ Cover bowl and let stand overnight./
The next day, mix ingredients again and fill casings./ Place sausage in freezer./

Saltimbocca Alla Romana

Serves 6

12 veal scallops
1 tsp. salt
¼ tsp. pepper, freshly
  ground
12 slices imported prosciutto
  ham
4 tbls. butter
2 tbls. shallots or scallions,
  minced
¾ cup marsala wine
1½ cups brown sauce
2 tbls. lemon juice
2 tbls. parsley, minced
Salt
Cayenne
1 lb. fresh or 2 packages
  frozen chopped spinach
4 eggs, hard-boiled and
  sliced

Between 2 pieces of wax paper, pound veal scallops very thin, then cut into 6 inch squares./ Season with salt and pepper./ Cover each piece of veal with a slice of ham and fasten with toothpicks./ In a frying pan, melt butter and brown veal over high heat on both sides./ Remove veal to oven-proof platter./ Add shallots to frying pan and cook until transparent./ Add wine and continue cooking until reduced by half./ Add brown sauce, lemon juice, parsley, salt and pepper to taste and heat sauce thoroughly./

In a buttered baking dish, spread spinach./ Arrange veal, ham side up, over spinach./ Remove toothpicks./ Place egg slices over ham and pour sauce on top./ In a 400° F. oven, bake for 15 minutes./

La Stella Restaurant

Hamburger Roulade

Serves 4

1 tbls. drippings
1 medium onion, chopped
1 small clove garlic, crushed
1 lb. ground chuck beef
1 egg, lightly beaten
2 slices bread, crust removed
Water
1 tsp. salt
¼ tsp. oregano, rosemary or
  basil
Pepper, freshly ground
2 tbls. dry bread crumbs
2 cups seasoned mashed
  potatoes
1 tbls. parsley, minced
3 strips bacon, (optional)

In a frying pan, sauté onion and garlic in drippings until onion is transparent./ In a mixing bowl, combine onion and garlic with ground beef, and egg./ Soften bread in water, pressing out excess liquid, and add to meat./ Add salt, oregano and pepper to taste and mix well./

Sprinkle a piece of wax paper with bread crumbs./ Press meat out on crumbs, forming a rectangle about ½ inch thick./ Combine mashed potatoes with parsley and spread on top of meat./ (If leftover potato is used, reheat in double boiler before using.)/ Roll the meat and potato filling like a jelly roll, using the wax paper as an aid./ Place roll in a shallow baking pan, which has been greased if meat is very lean./ Brush top of roll with additional drippings or top with bacon if desired./ In a 350° F. oven, bake approximately one hour, basting at least once during cooking./ Serve with a brown sauce made from pan drippings, or with mushroom or tomato sauce./

Tenderloin Beef Tip A La Chasseur

Serves 8

Fat
3 lbs. tenderloin beef tips,
  cut in long strips
1 medium onion, diced
½ lb. mushrooms (or 1
  medium can), sliced
1 clove garlic, minced
1 cup Burgundy wine
3 cups beef stock
2 tsp. salt
½ tsp. pepper, freshly
  ground
1-33 oz. can whole tomatoes,
  crushed with knife or fork
2 tbls. cornstarch
3 tbls. cold water

In a skillet, melt a few tablespoons fat and sauté beef tips quickly, until lightly brown./ Remove beef from skillet./ In the same pan, sauté onion, mushrooms, and garlic until lightly brown./ Add wine, and cook until liquid is reduced by half./

Add beef stock, salt, and pepper to skillet./ Add meat and tomatoes./ Cover skillet and simmer slowly for 45 minutes./ Mix cornstarch with cold water, and add to boiling liquid, stirring constantly./

(As a variation, chuck or round beef, cut in strips one inch long by ⅛ inch wide, may be used instead of tenderloin.)/

Chef: Mr. Hazy   Olympic Hotel

Meat Cholent

Serves 8 to 10

2 cups dried lima beans
Water
3 tbls. fat
3 lbs. beef brisket
3 onions, diced
2 tsp. salt
¼ tsp. pepper
¼ tsp. ground ginger
1 cup pearl barley
2 tbls. barley
2 tbls. flour
2 tsp. paprika

Soak beans in water to cover for 12 hours./ Drain beans./ In a heavy skillet, melt fat and brown the meat and onions./ Sprinkle meat with salt, pepper, and ginger, and then add the beans and barley, sprinkling everything with flour and paprika./ Add boiling water to one inch over top of mixture and cover skillet tightly./

In a 250° F. oven, bake the cholent 24 hours./ Alternatively, for faster cooking, bake in a 350° F. oven 4 to 5 hours./ Serve the meat sliced, with barley and beans./

Bean-Burger Meat Casserole

Serves 4

1 lb. ground round beef
1 tsp. salt
¼ tsp. pepper
1 tbls. butter
⅔ cup catsup
½ cup brown sugar
1 medium-large can baked
  beans
1 medium onion, thinly
  sliced
2 to 3 strips bacon

In a skillet, sauté meat and salt and pepper in butter until brown./ Combine catsup and brown sugar and mix well./ In a flat casserole, make two alternate layers of meat, beans, onions, and the catsup and brown sugar mixture./ Top layers with bacon strips./

In a 350°F. oven, bake casserole 30 to 40 minutes./ Casserole may be prepared ahead, covered with wrap, and refrigerated until baking time./

Duke's Chinese Steak

Serves 2

1-16 oz. sirloin steak
1 tbls. peanut oil
3 cups boktoi, chopped
½ cup water chestnuts,
  sliced
½ cup bamboo shoots,
  sliced
½ cup mushrooms, sliced
½ cup snow peas
3 cups chicken broth
1 clove garlic, crushed
1 tbls. sherry wine
2 tbls. monosodium
  glutamate
2 tbls. soy sauce
½ tbls. salt
½ tbls. sugar
2 tbls. cornstarch
¼ cup cold water

Broil steak to desired degree of doneness, and place on heated platter./ In a heavy skillet or wok, add oil and heat over high heat until oil cracks./ Add boktoi, water chestnuts, bamboo shoots, mushrooms, and snow peas to skillet./ Stir vegetables for one minute, and then add chicken broth./ Blend garlic and wine with vegetables./ Let mixture simmer for 3 minutes, stirring constantly./ Add monosodium glutamate, soy sauce, salt, and sugar./ Mix cornstarch with cold water, and add this to sauce, stirring until sauce comes to a boil./ Simmer for 2 minutes./

Serve steak on heated platter, covered with vegetables and sauce./

Duke's Restaurant

Sauerbraten

Serves 10 to 12

1 tbls. seasoned salt
½ tsp. pepper (optional)
2 carrots, thinly sliced
2 large onions, thinly sliced
2 large stalks celery with
  leaves, diced
4 whole cloves
4 whole black peppercorns
1 cup red wine vinegar
4 bay leaves
1-6 to 8 lb. roast beef
2 tbls. oil (or margarine)
2¼ tsp. arrowroot
2 tbls. sugar (or equivalent
  artificial sweetner)
10 crushed gingersnaps
1½ tbls. molasses

A day or two in advance, in a large glass bowl, combine salt, pepper, if desired, carrot, onion, celery, cloves, peppercorns, vinegar, and bay leaves./ Place beef in marinade, and spoon mixture over, covering meat on all sides./ Cover bowl and refrigerate, turning beef occasionally./

Remove beef when ready to cook./ In Dutch oven, heat oil or margarine, and brown beef./ Add marinade, cover pot, and simmer, for approximately 3 hours./

In a separate pan, combine arrowroot, sugar, and some liquid from marinade and blend till smooth./ Add to Dutch oven./ Continue simmering, covered, until beef is fork tender./

Remove beef from pot./ Into mixture in Dutch oven, stir crushed gingersnaps and molasses and cook until thickened./ Remove bay leaves and put mixture through food mill./ Let stand, and then skim off fat./

Slice beef./ Return beef and sauce to clean Dutch oven and heat./ To serve, arrange slices of beef on heated platter and spoon sauce over./

Kosher Spareribs

Serves 4

4 to 4½ lbs. breast of lamb
  riblets
1 onion, sliced thinly
1 lemon, sliced thinly

Barbecue Sauce

½ cup catsup
½ cup water
¼ cup vinegar
2 tbls. sugar
1 tbls. Worcestershire sauce
1 tsp. chili powder
1 tsp. hot sauce
1 tsp. dry mustard
⅛ tsp. salt
⅛ tsp. pepper
2 cloves garlic, minced
1 stalk celery, diced
  (optional)
¼ green pepper, diced
  (optional)

In a 9 by 13 inch pan, place ribs and cover with onion and lemon./ In a 450° F. oven, bake ribs for ½ to ¾ hour./ Drain fat from pan./

Prepare barbecue sauce by combining all ingredients and mixing well./ Pour barbecue sauce over ribs, and bake them in a 350° F. oven for one hour, turning ribs occasionally./

Gypsy Porkchops

Serves 8

16-½ inch thick loin
  pork chops
Salt
Pepper
1 clove garlic, peeled,
  crushed, and chopped
6 tbls. butter
Flour
4 tbls. fat
3 or 4 large onions, cubed
1 packet vegetable bouillon

Sprinkle chops with salt and pepper, and lay them on a board./ Mix garlic with butter and spread mixture on one side of each chop./ Lightly sprinkle flour on top of garlic butter./

In a skillet, heat fat, and sauté onion cubes until they are very lightly browned./ Remove onion from skillet and spread in large covered baking pan./ Place pan in a 375° F. oven./

Remove remaining fat from same skillet, and heat skillet until very hot./ Place chops in skillet side by side, floured side up, and brown./ Turn chops and brown floured side./ As chops are browned, place them on top of browned onions in oven pan./ When all chops are browned, cover pan and continue to bake 2 hours, turning chops after one hour./ If necessary, add a little water or stock to prevent sticking./

Transfer the chops to a warm platter./ Add vegetable bouillon to sauce and stir./ Pour sauce over chops./

Slavia Mt. Resort

Barbecued Pork

Serves 16 to 18

12 to 14 lb. fresh ham, with
  some fat removed
Garlic granules
Onion granules
Salt
Pepper
1 cup onion, diced
1 cup celery, diced
1 cup carrots, diced
1 quart water

Season ham with garlic granules, onion granules, salt and pepper to taste./ Arrange onion, celery and carrots in a roasting pan and place ham on top./ Add water to pan./ In a 350°F. oven, roast for 4 to 4½ hours./ Remove ham from oven, strain drippings and reserve, using to prepare barbecue sauce as directed below./

Barbecue Sauce

Drippings from fresh ham
2-14 oz. bottles catsup
2-12 oz. bottles chili sauce
1 lb. jar honey
Juice of 2 lemons
1 tbls. granulated onion
1 tbls. granulated garlic
1 tbls. chili powder
1 tbls. dry mustard
1½ tsp. Worcestershire
  sauce
Salt to taste
Pepper to taste
Few drops of Tabasco

Refrigerate drippings, allowing fat to solidify./ Remove and discard fat./ In a large saucepan, combine drippings and remaining ingredients./ Bring to a boil, reduce heat and simmer sauce for 5 minutes./

Slice ham approximately ¼ inch thick and serve with sauce./

Danny's Fair Acres Restaurant

Game

Roast Pheasant

Serves 2

1 pheasant
Salt
Pepper
Butter
2 to 3 bacon slices
½ cup heavy cream
1 tbls. flour
1 cup beef (or chicken) stock

Rub pheasant inside and out with salt and pepper./ Place breast side up in roasting pan or casserole, and dot with butter./ Place bacon slices across breast./ In a 350° F. oven, roast pheasant approximately one hour, basting with butter./ Add a little water if necessary./ Pour cream over bird, and return to oven for several minutes./

Remove pheasant from casserole, and keep warm./ Add flour to pan drippings and blend until smooth./ Stir in stock, and continue to stir until gravy thickens slightly./ Season with salt to taste./

Venison Collops

Serves 6

2 tbls. butter
2 tbls. onion, chopped
1½ tbls. flour
1 cup beef broth
Salt
Pepper
⅓ cup currant jelly
6 slices cold, cooked venison
2 tbls. sherry
1 cup rice, cooked

In a heavy skillet, heat butter and chopped onion./ When onion starts to brown, stir in flour./ Gradually add beef broth, stirring, until sauce is thickened and smooth./ Season with salt and pepper to taste./ Add currant jelly and mix thoroughly./ Place venison slices in sauce and heat through./ When meat is hot, add sherry./ Serve with rice./

Venison Burgers

Serves 8

2 lbs. ground venison
1 large onion, chopped
1 tbls. Worcestershire sauce
1 clove garlic, finely
  chopped
2 tsp. dry mustard
Salt
Freshly ground black pepper
¼ cup oil

In a bowl, combine venison, onion, Worcestershire sauce, garlic, mustard and salt and pepper to taste./ Shape into patties./ In a skillet, heat oil and fry patties slowly until cooked through and browned./

Venison Pepper Steak

Serves 6 to 8

2 venison steaks, cut into ½"
  strips
2 tbls. vegetable oil
1 large onion, sliced
1 small can sliced
  mushrooms
1 can mushroom gravy
Water, measured in
  mushroom gravy can
Salt
Pepper
Garlic powder
2 large green peppers, cut
  into strips

In a large skillet, brown venison strips in oil./ Add onion to skillet, and sauté quickly./ When onions are brown, add mushrooms, gravy and water, and salt, pepper, and garlic powder to taste./ Add green pepper to skillet./ Simmer 1½ hours./ Serve venison pepper steak over rice./

Pheasant

Serves 2

Juice of 1 lemon
½ cup butter
½ cup cranberries
Salt
Pepper
1 pheasant
6 strips bacon
2 tbls. whiskey
½ cup port wine (or claret)

Mix lemon juice with a walnut-sized piece of butter, cranberries and salt and pepper./

Wrap the pheasant with bacon strips, and place in a roasting pan./ Pour whiskey over pheasant./ Add remaining butter and cranberry mixture to the pan./ In a 400° F. oven, cook the pheasant for 20 minutes./ Add wine, and baste well./ Return pan to oven for 35 to 45 minutes./ Remove pheasant, discarding bacon strips, and keep warm./ Pour gravy and pan drippings into saucepan, and cook until thickened on top of stove./ Serve gravy separately./

(This recipe can be used with partridge, reducing final cooking time in proportion to the size of the bird.)/

Roast Stuffed Wild Turkey

Serves 8 to 10

1-12 lb. turkey, cleaned,
  washed and dried
Salt
Pepper
Garlic powder
Poultry seasoning
Paprika
Butter or margarine, softened

Sprinkle inside of turkey with salt and pepper./ In a bowl, cream butter or margarine with salt, pepper, garlic powder, poultry seasoning and paprika to taste./ Stuff turkey cavity lightly with stuffing, prepared as directed below./ Sew or skewer skin together, if desired./ Twist wing tips under back to hold in place./ Tie legs together securely if necessary./ Rub butter paste over outside of turkey and place on rack set in roasting pan./ In a 425° F. oven, roast turkey, breast side down, until browned, about 20 minutes./

Turn, and roast breast side up, until that side is browned./ (If turkey is too large to turn, roast breast side up and brown that side only.)/ Baste turkey with pan drippings./ Reduce oven to 375° F., cover turkey with tin foil, tightly crimped around roasting pan edges, and continue cooking until bird is done./ Allow 20 minutes per pound for roasting./ Let turkey sit for 20 minutes after cooking time for easier carving./ Serve with giblet gravy./

Ritz Cracker Stuffing

½ cup onion, sautéed
1 box Ritz crackers, finely
  crushed
2 eggs, beaten
1 cup cold water
½ lb. pistachio nuts, shelled
  (or ½ cup pine nuts)
  (optional)
½ cup celery, diced
1 large carrot, grated
1 tbls. parsley, chopped
Salt
Pepper

In a bowl, blend onions into crushed crackers./ Add beaten eggs and mix well./ Add remaining ingredients and blend thoroughly./

Giblet Gravy

Giblets from
  1 wild turkey
Salted water
Pan drippings from roast
  turkey
¼ cup flour
½ cup cream (optional)
Salt
Pepper

In a saucepan, simmer giblets in salted water to cover until tender./ Drain, reserving broth./ Cool giblets and chop./ In another saucepan, pour 4 tablespoons pan drippings (add enough butter, if necessary, to equal 4 tablespoons fat)./ Pour 2 cups giblet broth into drippings in roasting pan and scrape loose brown particles (add enough water to equal 2 cups liquid, if necessary)./ Add flour to drippings in saucepan and cook, stirring, until browned./ Gradually add giblet broth and cook, stirring, until thickened./ Add cream, if desired, and season with salt and pepper to taste./ Reheat if necessary./

Pilgrim's Rabbit Stew

Serves 4

1 rabbit or hare
½ cup vinegar
½ cup water
1 medium onion, sliced
2 tsp. lemon juice
6 to 8 peppercorns
1 whole clove
1 bay leaf
Salt
Pepper
4 tbls. butter (or oil)
½ onion, chopped
4 tbls. flour

Two days before serving, cut up rabbit with giblets./ Mix together vinegar, water, onion, lemon juice, peppercorns, clove, bay leaf, and salt and pepper to taste./ Pour this mixture over rabbit, and marinate in a cool place for 2 days./

Drain and dry each piece of marinated rabbit, reserving liquid./ In a large skillet melt butter and lightly fry rabbit pieces with chopped onion./ Add flour to skillet, and cook until flour browns./ Add ½ cup of marinade to the meat./ Cover the skillet and stew approximately 1½ hour, or until rabbit is tender./ Add more liquid if marinade cooks away./

Venison Bourguignon

Serves 8 to 10

4 tbls. butter (or salt pork)
1 clove garlic, minced
1 large onion, sliced
1 carrot, sliced
6 lbs. boneless roast of venison
2 cups dry red wine
Salt
Pepper
Bouquet garni (½ bay leaf, 2 sprigs fresh thyme, 3 sprigs fresh parsley)
¼ lb. bacon, cut in small pieces
2 tbls. flour
½ lb. mushrooms, sliced
20 small onions, frozen or canned (or fresh onions, parboiled)
2 oz. brandy

In a Dutch Oven, melt butter or salt pork./ Add garlic, onion, and carrot, and cook for several minutes./ Place venison roast in Dutch oven and brown on all sides./ Add wine, salt and pepper to taste, and bouquet garni./ Cover and simmer venison 2 to 3 hours, until meat is tender./ Remove meat for carving./

In frying pan, cook chopped bacon and drain on paper towel./ Skim fat from liquid in Dutch oven./ Thicken liquid with flour./ Add bacon, mushrooms, onions, and brandy to Dutch oven, and simmer while carving venison./ Return venison slices to gravy./ Reheat venison, and serve on heated platter./

Poultry

Chicken With Paprika

Serves 6 to 8

2 tbls. butter
2 tbls. vegetable oil
2 broiler-fryer chickens,
   cut up
Salt
Pepper
3 medium onions, chopped
1 clove garlic, chopped
2 tbls. paprika, preferably
   Hungarian
2½ tbls. flour
1 cup chicken broth
2 cups sour cream, room
   temperature

In a casserole, heat butter and oil./ Brown pieces of chicken in casserole, then season with salt and pepper to taste and remove./

In the remaining fat, cook onion and garlic until onion is transparent./ Add paprika and flour to casserole, and cook ingredients for 3 minutes, stirring gently./ Add broth and then sour cream to the mixture./ Stir sauce constantly until it is smooth and thickened./

Replace chicken in casserole./ (At this point, cooking can be interrupted./ Refrigerate the casserole, and increase the baking time when cooking is resumed.)/ Cover the casserole and bake in a preheated 350° F. oven for one hour, or until chicken is tender./

Serve chicken with noodles or potato pancakes and mixed green salad./

Roast Duckling With Sauerkraut

Serves 4

6 dried mushrooms
Water
1-4 to 5 lb. duckling
Salt
Pepper
2 large onions, chopped
2 tbls. fat (bacon drippings or
   lard)
2 tbls. paprika
2 lbs. sauerkraut, drained
1 cup green peppers, cored,
   seeded and chopped
½ tsp. dried thyme
1½ cups tomato juice

In a bowl, soak mushrooms in lukewarm water to cover for 20 minutes, then drain, pressing out all liquid./ Slice mushrooms and set aside, reserving the liquid./

Wash duckling, pat dry and sprinkle with salt and pepper to taste./ Prick skin in several places with fork./ In a roasting pan, in a 325° F. oven, roast duck for 1½ hours./

While duckling is cooking, sauté onions in fat in a saucepan./ Add paprika and cook one minute./ Add sauerkraut, mushrooms, peppers and thyme and stir./ Pour in reserved mushroom liquid and tomato juice and season with salt and pepper to taste./ Cook mixture on low heat, covered, for 30 minutes./

Remove duckling from roasting pan and place on platter./ Spoon off all but 2 tablespoons of fat in roasting pan and add sauerkraut mixture to drippings, mixing./ Place duckling over sauerkraut, return pan to oven and bake another 30 to 45 minutes, until tender./ Cut up duckling into serving pieces and serve surrounded by sauerkraut mixture./

Ducklings A L'Orange

Serves 4 to 6

2-5 pound ducklings,
  dressed
Lemon juice
Salt
2 bay leaves
1 cup chicken stock
1 cup bitter orange
  marmalade
½ cup honey
½ cup port wine
¼ cup red wine vinegar
2 cloves garlic, crushed
½ tsp. tarragon
⅛ tsp. rosemary
Orange halves (or kumquats)

Wipe ducklings with a damp cloth./ Sprinkle generously all over with lemon juice and salt./ Tuck bay leaves in cavities./ In an uncovered roasting pan, in a 350° F. oven, roast ducklings until they are golden./ Pour off fat./ Cool ducklings, and quarter them./ Discard bay leaves./ Return quartered ducklings to roasting pan, cut side down, without overlapping./ (This can be done the day before serving./ Refrigerate quartered ducklings.)/

While ducklings are roasting, prepare the sauce./ In a pan over medium flame, combine chicken stock, marmalade, honey, wine, vinegar, garlic, tarragon, and rosemary until sauce is well blended./

Pour sauce over quartered ducklings./ Cover roasting pan and bake ducklings in a 300° F. oven for one hour./ Uncover pan and continue cooking, basting ducklings, about 15 minutes, or until they are a rich brown./ Serve garnished with orange or kumquats./

Chicken Giblets With Meatballs

Serves 4 to 6

4 tbls. chicken fat
1 stalk celery, diced
1 onion, diced
1 carrot, diced
1 clove garlic, minced
Giblets (gizzards, necks, and
  wings) of 6 chickens
3 tsp. salt
½ tsp. pepper, freshly
  ground
2 tbls. flour
2 cups beef broth
2 cups canned whole
  tomatoes
1 lb. ground beef
3 tbls. cold water
¼ tsp. garlic powder

In a large saucepan, heat the chicken fat and brown celery, onion, carrot, and garlic in it./ Add giblets to the pan and brown them for 5 minutes./ Sprinkle with 2 teaspoons salt, ¼ teaspoon pepper, and 2 tbls. flour./ Bring the beef broth to a boil and add it to the mixture./ Add tomatoes./ Cover saucepan and simmer for one hour./

Mix together beef, water, one teaspoon salt, and garlic powder, and form into small balls./ Add to the giblets and cook an additional 20 minutes./ This recipe can be served with egg barley or rice./

Singer's Restaurant

Charles Chicken Breast Supreme

Serves 6

¼ cup butter
6 chicken breasts, boned,
  skinned, and halved
¼ cup sliced mushrooms
  (or 1 can mushroom
  pieces, drained)
¼ cup white wine
1 cup sour cream
1 can mushroom soup,
  undiluted
Paprika

In a large skillet, melt butter and brown chicken breasts on both sides until they are delicately brown./ Place them in a large baking dish, one layer thick./

Sauté mushrooms in the skillet for 5 minutes, adding more butter if needed./ Add white wine, sour cream, and mushroom soup./ Blend ingredients well, including drippings in the bottom of the skillet, until mixture is smooth./

Pour mixture over the chicken./ In a 350° F. oven bake for one hour./ Sprinkle chicken with paprika, and serve with wild rice or long grained white rice./

Roark's Tavern

Chicken Au Champagne

Serves 6 to 8

2-2½ lb. fryers, disjointed
2 tsp. salt
¼ tsp. pepper, freshly
  ground
½ cup butter
1½ cups champagne
3 tbls. lemon juice
2 tbls. Curacao (orange
  liqueur)
Oranges, sliced
Seedless green grapes

Wash and dry the chicken pieces and season with salt and pepper./ In a deep skillet, melt half the butter./ Sauté the chicken in it until browned and tender./ Add champagne, lemon juice and Curacao to the skillet./ Shake the skillet over low heat until chicken is glazed with the sauce./ Add remaining butter to the skillet./

Arrange chicken on hot platter, pour sauce over it, and garnish with orange slices and grapes./

Chicken Curry

Serves 4

1-2 lb. fryer chicken
3 tsp. curry powder
Salt
Pepper
1 tbls. olive oil
1 medium onion, sliced
2 bananas, sliced
1 apple, sliced and cubed
2 cloves garlic, diced
1-8 oz. can crushed
  pineapple
1 tbls. flour
½ tsp. paprika
1 cup chicken broth

Cut chicken into pieces, and sprinkle it with 2 teaspoons curry powder and salt and pepper to taste./ In a large saucepan, heat oil and fry the chicken until it is brown./ Remove chicken from the pan./

Add onion, banana, apple, garlic, pineapple, flour, one teaspoon curry powder and paprika to pan, and heat until ingredients are hot./ Return chicken to pan and add broth./ Cover the pan, and simmer it approximately one hour, or until the chicken is tender./

Serve with rice and chutney./

Chateau Special Chicken

Serves 6

2 eggs, beaten
1 cup flour
1 tsp. salt
½ cup water
3 chicken breasts, skinned
   and boned
Peanut oil
3 cups bok toi (or Chinese
   cabbage)
1 cup water chestnuts, sliced
1 cup bamboo shoots, sliced
½ cup Chinese black
   mushrooms, sliced
½ lb. snow peas
¼ cup sherry wine
¼ tsp. pepper
⅛ tsp. garlic, chopped
½ cup chicken stock
1½ tsp. monosodium
   glutamate
3 tbls. cornstarch

Combine eggs, flour, and ½ teaspoon salt in ¼ cup water./ Pound and flatten chicken breasts into cutlets./ Dip cutlets in flour mixture until they are well coated./ In a skillet, heat 2 inches of oil to 375° F. and fry cutlets 3 minutes on each side./ Drain cutlets and keep them hot./

In a wok or deep skillet, heat ¼ cup oil and add bok toi, water chestnuts, bamboo shoots, mushrooms, snow peas, wine, pepper, garlic, and ½ teaspoon salt./ Stir and toss mixture./ Add chicken stock and simmer 3 or 4 minutes./ Add monosodium glutamate to wok./ Mix cornstarch with ¼ cup water to a smooth consistency./ Add this slowly to the mixture, constantly stirring until a desirable consistency is obtained./

Place all vegetables with sauce on a large dish and top with chicken cutlets./

Chateau Restaurant

Chicken Kiev

Serves 6

3 whole chicken breasts,
   boned and halved
½ cup margarine
Salt
Black pepper, freshly ground
2 tbls. chopped chives
Flour
2 eggs, lightly beaten
1 cup fresh bread crumbs
Oil

Place chicken breasts between wax paper and pound until thin with a mallet or the flat side of a butcher knife./ Do not split flesh./

Cut margarine into finger shaped pieces./ Place a piece in the middle of each breast, sprinkle with salt and pepper to taste and chopped chives and roll up envelope fashion with sides overlapping./ Dredge each roll lightly in flour, then dip into beaten egg and roll in bread crumbs./ Refrigerate one hour./

In a heavy skillet, heat enough oil or fat to cover rolls./ When temperature of fat reaches 360° F., add chicken rolls and brown on all sides./ Drain on absorbent paper./ (If wing bones are still attached, place a paper frill on each.)/

Brown's Hotel

Chicken Hoisin

Serves 3

3 boneless chicken breasts
1 tbls. sherry

Cube chicken, mix it with sherry, soy sauce, and cornstarch, and set it aside./

1 tbls. soy sauce
1 tbls. cornstarch
4 tbls. oil
½ cup water chestnuts,
   drained
½ cup mushrooms, sliced
½ cup green pepper,
   cut into small pieces
2 tbls. Hoisin sauce*
⅓ cup almonds (or
   cashew nuts)

Heat a wok or large skillet on high heat, and add one tablespoon oil./ When oil is hot, add and stir fry water chestnuts, mushrooms, and green pepper for 3 minutes./ Remove vegetables from wok./

Add and heat 3 tablespoons oil in wok./ Stir fry the chicken in wok approximately 3 minutes, or until chicken is white./ Add vegetables, Hoisin sauce, and nuts to the wok./ Serve chicken with rice./

*available at Chinese groceries or gourmet shops.

Southern Fried Chicken

Serves 6 to 8

2 small broiler chickens
Salt
Pepper
1½ cups milk
2 eggs
3 cups flour
1 tsp. salt
⅛ tsp. pepper
⅛ tsp. garlic powder
⅛ tsp. poultry seasoning
⅛ tsp. monosodium glutamate
⅛ tsp. paprika
Vegetable shortening

Disjoint, wash, and dry chickens./ Season them with salt and pepper to taste./ Mix milk with eggs./ Mix 1½ cups of flour with salt, pepper, garlic powder, poultry seasoning, monosodium glutamate and paprika./ Dip chicken in remaining 1½ cups flour, then in milk and egg mixture, and then in seasoned flour./

In a heavy skillet, add vegetable shortening for deep frying, and heat to 375° F./ Add chicken to skillet and brown on all sides./

Broiler Chickens In Wine Sauce

Serves 6 to 8

1 large onion, sliced
2 broiler chickens
½ cup margarine
½ cup white wine
2 cloves garlic, crushed
½ tsp. salt
½ tsp. rubbed sage

In the bottom of a roasting pan, lay sliced onions and place chicken on top./ (Chicken may be stuffed if desired.)/

Melt margarine in small skillet./ Remove skillet from heat and add wine, garlic, salt, and sage./ Brush the mixture over chicken./ In a 400° F. oven, roast chickens one hour or more, according to their size, until golden./ Baste chickens occasionally./ Reserve pan drippings./

Currant Gravy Sauce

3 tbls. flour
1 cup white wine
1 cup currant jelly
1 tbls. dry mustard
1 tsp. salt

Pour off drippings from roasting pan./ Place 3 tablespoons of drippings in a saucepan, gradually adding the flour and stirring the mixture until smooth./ Add wine, jelly, mustard, and salt to saucepan, and bring to boil./ Serve with chickens./

Mamaliga With Chicken Livers (*Romanian Corn Meal*) *Serves 6 to 8*

2 cups yellow corn meal
1 cup cold water
2 tsp. salt
¼ tsp. white pepper
3 cups boiling water
10 tbls. sweet butter (or
 7⅓ tbls. rendered chicken
 fat)
1½ lbs. whole chicken livers
2 tbls. onion, minced finely
¼ tsp. black pepper

In a saucepan, blend cornmeal, 1½ teaspoons salt, and white pepper with cold water until a smooth paste is formed./ Gradually add the boiling water to paste stirring well to prevent lumps./ Cook over low heat for 30 minutes, stirring continually./ Add 8 tablespoons butter or 5⅓ tablespoons chicken fat, and blend thoroughly to make Mamaliga./

In a skillet, melt remaining 2 tablespoons butter or fat, and lightly sauté onions./ Add chicken livers to skillet, and cook turning with wooden spoon./ Sprinkle with ½ teaspoon salt and black pepper./ When livers have lost their pinkness, pile them on top of Mamaliga and serve./

Breast of Chicken Parmagiana *Serves 3 to 4*

2½ lbs. boneless chicken
 breasts
Salt
Pepper
Monosodium glutamate
1 cup bread crumbs
2 eggs, beaten
Butter or oil
Tomato meat sauce
Mozzarella cheese, sliced

Place chicken breasts between 2 pieces of wax paper and pound with the bottom of a small iron fry pan to flatten./ Season chicken with salt, pepper and monosodium glutamate to taste./ Dip into beaten eggs, then bread crumbs, taking care to coat all surfaces./

In a heavy frying pan, heat butter and sauté chicken on all sides until golden brown./ Remove chicken to baking pan, pour meat sauce over and top with sliced cheese./ In a 375° F. oven, bake chicken until cheese is melted./

Chef: William Bott *Monticello Raceway*

Goose With Garlic Sauce *Serves 6*

1-12 lb. goose, cut up
3 onions, sliced
1 cup celery, chopped
1 carrot, sliced
4 tsp. salt
8 peppercorns, crushed
½ tsp. dried tarragon
½ tsp. dried thyme
4 cups milk
12 cloves garlic, peeled
4 egg yolks
½ cup parsley, chopped

In a saucepan, place goose with onions, celery, carrot, 2 teaspoons salt, peppercorns, tarragon, thyme and water to cover./ Bring water to boil, cover, reduce heat and simmer for one hour or until goose is tender./ Remove goose and keep warm./

In top of double boiler, scald 3 cups of milk./ Add garlic./ Beat egg yolks with remaining one cup milk and stir into scalded milk./ Add remaining 2 teaspoons salt./ Place pot over hot water and cook, stirring constantly, until sauce is thickened./ To serve, pour sauce over goose and garnish generously with chopped parsley./

Eggs and Cheese

BOB LONGO '75

Swiss Apple Pancakes

Yield: 12 pancakes

8 eggs
4 cups milk
4 cups flour
½ cup sugar
4 medium baking apples,
  peeled, cored, and thinly
  sliced
¾ cup raisins
Butter
Cinnamon sugar

Beat eggs./ Add milk, flour, and sugar to eggs and beat mixture well./ Mix apples and raisins together./ Heat 2 tablespoons butter in a 7 inch frying pan until medium hot./ Ladle ¾ cup of batter into pan, and spread some apple-raisin mixture on top./

Fry pancake until it is golden brown./ Transfer pancake to greased cookie sheet, sprinkle with cinnamon sugar, and dot with butter./ Repeat with rest of batter and apple-raisin mixture./ Place cookie sheet in a 350° F. oven for 10 to 15 minutes, or until pancakes puff up./

Chef: Danny Kuen   Kutsher's Country Club

Swiss Omelette

Serves 4

5 slices bacon, diced
Butter
3 to 4 potatoes, boiled,
  peeled, and diced
1 onion, chopped
1 tomato, chopped (or 1
  green pepper, chopped)
8 eggs
1¼ cups Emmenthaler (or
  Swiss Gruyére) cheese,
  grated
Salt
Pepper

Slowly fry bacon in large frying pan, then drain it./ Melt butter in pan and add potato, onion, and tomato or green pepper cooking until vegetables are tender and lightly browned./ Mix thoroughly eggs, cheese, and salt and pepper to taste and pour over ingredients in pan./

As the omelette cooks, lift its edges with a spatula, letting uncooked egg run under./ Repeat this process until all the liquid is used./ Place omelette under broiler until cheese is melted and lightly browned./

Egg Pizza

Serves 4

6 eggs
½ tbls. Parmesan cheese,
  grated
½ tsp. salt
4 oz. tomato sauce
½ tsp. sugar
Garlic salt
½ cup mozzarella cheese,
  grated
½ tsp. oregano

Mix eggs with Parmesan cheese and salt and place in an electric frying pan set at 350° F./ Cover pan and cook eggs approximately 3 minutes, or until just set on top./ Do not stir./

Mix tomato sauce with sugar and a pinch of garlic salt./ Spread tomato sauce over eggs, and sprinkle top with mozzarella cheese and oregano./ Recover pan, and cook approximately 2 minutes, or until cheese has started to melt./

Fresh Fruit Omelette

Serves 4

10 eggs
¼ cup cream, milk or water
Salt
Pepper
Parsley, chopped
2 cups diced fresh
 fruit—combine at least 4 of
 the following:
 oranges
 apples
 pears
 seedless grapes
 peaches
 bananas
 blueberries
 strawberries
 melon
4 oz. Jack-type
 cheese—Caljack, Monterey
 Jack, etc., cut lengthwise
 into 4 strips
Butter or margarine

Mix eggs, liquid, and salt, pepper and parsley to taste./ In an 8 inch skillet, melt shortening./ Pour ¼ of egg mixture into pan, lifting edges as it cooks so liquid from center can run down and under./ Spoon ½ cup fruit and 1 strip of cheese into center and fold omelette over./ Heat through, then remove to warm ovenproof platter./ Place in 200° F. oven and keep warm./ Repeat process 3 times more with remaining ingredients./ Sprinkle omelettes with parsley before serving./

Cheese Blintzes

Yield: 12 to 14 blintzes

3 eggs
½ cup water
Sugar
Salt
Approximately ½ cup flour
Butter (or margarine)
½ lb. farmer cheese
⅓ cup cottage cheese
Cinnamon

Beat 2 eggs well, and combine with water and a dash each of sugar and salt./ Gradually add flour until a smooth batter is formed./ Grease a 7 inch cast iron or teflon frying pan with butter and heat./ Pour approximately 3 tablespoons batter into pan, just enough to cover bottom of pan./ Let batter set, and brown blintz lightly./ Fry on one side only./ Turn blintz out on smooth dish towel, brown side up./ Continue making blintzes until batter is used up, greasing pan each time./

To make filling, mix together farmer cheese, cottage cheese, one egg, 2 teaspoons sugar, one teaspoon salt, and a dash of cinnamon./ Place one tablespoon of filling on each blintz./ Fold over sides of blintz, and roll up./ (At this point, blintzes may be refrigerated or frozen for future use.)/ Fry blintzes in melted butter to a golden brown before serving./ Serve with sour cream or desired topping./

Swiss Cheese-Mushroom Pie

Serves 6

3 tbls. butter (or margarine)
1 cup onion, thinly sliced
1½ lbs. mushrooms, sliced
1 tbls. lemon juice
1 tsp. salt
½ tsp. Worcestershire sauce
Pepper
1 package pie crust mix
½ lb. Swiss cheese, grated or
finely cut
1 egg yolk
1 tbls. water

Melt butter in a skillet, add onion, and cook 2 minutes./ Add mushrooms, lemon juice, salt, Worcestershire sauce, and a dash of pepper./ Cook mixture 5 minutes, then drain./

Prepare pie crust as directed on package./ Roll ¾ of the dough into a 12 inch circle./ Fit dough into 9 inch pie pan, allowing one inch of dough to overhang./ Roll out remaining dough; cut into 8 to 10 ½ inch strips./

Combine mushroom mixture with cheese, and mix well./ Turn mixture into pastry shell./ Lattice pastry strips on top, trimming ends even with edge of shell./ Moisten and fold overhang over ends of strips./ Flute edge of pie./ Beat egg yolk and water, and brush over pastry./ In a 375° F. oven, bake pie 35 to 40 minutes, or until pastry is golden brown./ Serve pie hot or cold./

Grossinger's Cheese Strudel

Serves 12

Strudel Batter

4 eggs
1 cup water
¾ cup sifted flour
2 tbls. vegetable oil
½ tsp. salt
Butter (or oil) for frying

Cheese Filling

1½ lb. farmer cheese
¼ lb. cream cheese
¼ lb. sugar
2 egg yolks
2 tbls. cornstarch
Dash of vanilla
Rind of ½ lemon, grated
Rind of ½ orange, grated

Custard

4 cups sour cream
5 eggs
½ cup sugar
½ cup heavy cream

In three separate bowls, combine ingredients to form strudel batter, cheese filling, and custard./

Lightly grease and heat a large, ovenproof frying pan./ Pour in some strudel batter, tilting the pan so as to coat the entire surface with a thin layer of batter./ Place pan in a 400° F. oven and bake for 2 minutes./ Remove strudel leaf by turning pan upside down on a clean dish towel./ Spread cheese filling along one end of leaf and roll up./ Repeat entire process, using up all batter and filling./

In a buttered baking pan, lay strudels side by side./ Pour custard sauce over./ In a 325° F. oven bake for 45 minutes./ Cut strudels into squares and serve with stewed blueberries or sour cream./

Grossinger Hotel

Calico Egg Sandwich

Serves 4

4 eggs, hard-boiled, coarsely
  chopped
¾ cup cooked ham, diced
½ cup cheddar cheese,
  shredded
¼ cup mayonnaise
¼ cup celery, finely
  chopped
2 tbls. onion, finely chopped
½ tsp. dry mustard
½ tsp. salt
¼ tsp. pepper
4 large hard rolls, halved and
  buttered

Combine eggs, ham, cheese, mayonnaise, celery, onion, mustard, salt, and pepper, and mix well./ Place roll halves on a baking sheet and spoon mixture onto them./ In a 400° F. oven bake approximately 15 minutes, or until cheese starts to melt and edges are delicately browned./

Mini Fruit Omelette

Serves 1 or 2

3 eggs
3 tbls. water
½ tsp. salt
1 tbls. butter
½ cup fresh pineapple
  chunks, sugared (or ½ cup
  fresh strawberries, sliced
  and sugared)
2 tbls. powdered sugar

With a fork, mix eggs, water, and salt./ Heat butter in an 8 inch skillet or omelette pan, until butter is just hot enough to sizzle a drop of water./ Pour egg mixture into pan./ Mixture should set at edges at once./ As the eggs thicken, carefully draw thickened portions toward the center with a spatula or fork, so that uncooked portions flow to the bottom./ Tilt skillet to hasten flow of uncooked eggs./ Keep mixture as level as possible./

When eggs are set and surface still moist, increase heat to brown omelette bottom quickly./ To serve, put desired fruit in center of omelette and fold in half./ Sprinkle top half with powdered sugar./

Rice and Pasta

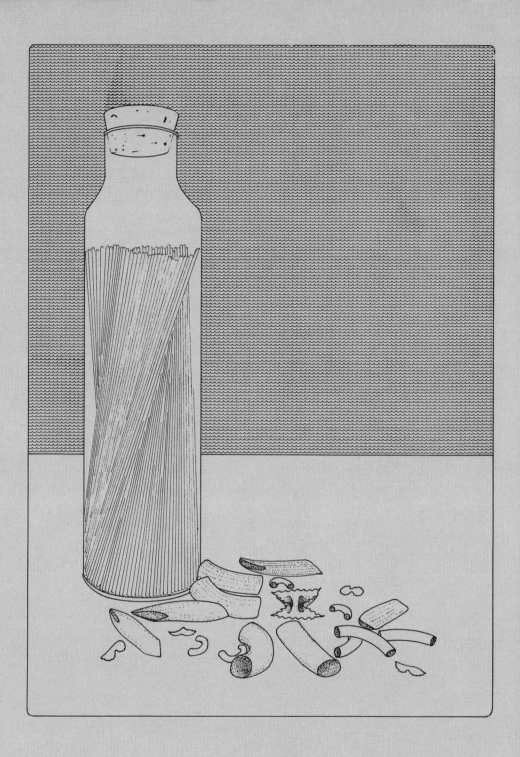

Stuffed Seashell Macaroni

Serves 10 to 12

3 tbls. butter
⅓ cup fresh mushrooms,
  sliced
3 tbls. flour
1½ cups hot milk
Salt
White pepper
½ cup green peas
1 lb. large pasta shells,
  cooked and drained
3 cups tomato meat sauce
½ cup grated Romano
  cheese

In a saucepan, heat butter, add mushrooms and sauté until tender./ Remove mushrooms from pan and set aside./ With a wire whisk, stir in flour and cook, stirring, until well blended./ Gradually add hot milk, stirring constantly with whisk until mixture is thickened and smooth./ Cook 2 minutes longer, then season with salt and pepper to taste./ Add mushrooms and green peas to sauce./

Fill pasta shells with vegetable mixture and place side by side in a large, greased baking pan./ Pour meat sauce over shells and sprinkle with grated cheese./ In a 400°F. oven, bake for 15 minutes, or until browned./

La Stella Restaurant

Apple Noodle Pudding

Serves 4

½ lb. noodles, cooked
3 apples, peeled, cored and
  sliced
1 cup cold water
1 cup sugar
½ cup raisins
4 eggs
¼ cup orange juice
3 tbls. lemon juice
1 tsp. vanilla
¼ tsp. salt
2 tbls. sugar
1 tsp. cinnamon
¼ tsp. nutmeg
Butter or margarine

In a large bowl, combine first 10 ingredients and mix well./ Turn into a well-greased 2 quart baking pan./ Combine sugar, cinnamon and nutmeg and sprinkle on top./ Dot with butter or margarine./ In a 350°F. oven, bake pudding for ¾ to one hour./

Pilaf

Serves 4 to 6

1 cup long grain rice
¼ cup butter
2 cups chicken broth
Scant ¼ cup pignole (pine
  nuts), browned (optional)
2 tbls. tomato sauce
Salt

Wash rice until rinse water is clear./ Melt butter in a pot with tightly fitting cover and sauté rice over medium-high heat for several minutes, stirring constantly, until rice grains are individually coated with butter./ Add chicken broth, pignoli, if desired, tomato sauce, and salt to taste./ Cover pot and cook over low heat for approximately 20 minutes, or until all broth is absorbed./ Remove pot from heat and let pilaf rest 15 minutes before serving./

Bolognese Spaghetti Sauce

Serves 4

¼ cup olive oil
½ cup butter
1 cup onions, finely chopped
1 lb. ground beef
4 strips bacon, finely
 chopped
3 tbls. parsley, finely
 chopped
4 cloves of garlic, finely
 chopped
1 tsp. salt
½ tsp. crushed red pepper
Black pepper
¼ cup red wine
1 cup canned tomatoes
1 cup tomato puree
2 tbls. tomato paste
2 stalks celery, finely
 chopped
1 carrot, finely chopped

In a saucepan over low heat, warm olive oil./ Melt butter in pan, add onion and sauté until golden brown./ Add ground beef and bacon and sauté until brown, stirring occasionally./ Add parsley, garlic, salt, red pepper and black pepper to taste./ Cook over low heat for approximately 10 minutes./ Add wine, cover, and cook for several minutes more./ Add tomatoes, tomato puree and tomato paste and bring to a boil./ Add celery and carrot./ Cover pan and cook over low heat for one hour, stirring occasionally./ Skim fat./

Perogi Or Kreplach

Yield: approximately 24

3 cups flour
1 tsp. baking powder
Salt
2 eggs
Water
1 package farmer cheese
2 quarts potatoes, boiled,
 peeled, and mashed
Pepper
Butter (or margarine)

In a large bowl, sift flour, baking powder, and ¼ teaspoon salt./ Add one well-beaten egg and approximately 1½ cups water, and mix ingredients well./ Roll dough out on floured board to about ¼ inch thick, and cut dough with floured glass rim./

Make filling by combining farmer cheese, mashed potatoes, one egg, and salt and pepper to taste./ Place a spoonful of filling on dough circle, fold circle in half and pinch edges together, lightly./

Lower perogi, a few at a time, into 2 quarts boiling salted water./ Immediately, lower heat and cook approximately 10 minutes./ Remove perogi with slotted spoon, rinse under water and place in buttered baking pan with butter between layers to prevent sticking./ In a 400°F. oven, bake for 15 minutes. (Alternately, after poaching, perogi may be fried in butter until golden brown.)/

Polenta And Cheese Casserole

Serves 6 to 8

4 cups water
2 tsp. salt
2 cups yellow corn meal (or
  Italian instant polenta)
3 tbls. bread crumbs
2¼ cups fontina (or
  mozzarella) cheese,
  coarsely grated
½ cup butter

In a heavy 2 quart pot, bring water to a boil./ Add salt to pot, then slowly whisk in cornmeal./ Cover pot tightly and cook cornmeal very slowly for 20 minutes, stirring frequently./

Grease a shallow baking dish, and sprinkle it with bread crumbs./ Spread a quarter of the cornmeal in it, cover with a quarter of the cheese and dot with a quarter of the butter./ Repeat the layers three more times./ In a 375°F. oven bake polenta for 15 minutes, or until it is browned./

Serve wedges of polenta with a meat sauce or tomato sauce with Parmesan cheese./

Kasha Varnitchkes

Serves 10

1 cup medium kasha (roasted
  brown buckwheat groats)
1 egg, well beaten
1 tsp. salt
1 tsp. garlic powder
2 cups boiling water
1 cup bow ties (noodles)
  cooked according to
  instructions on box
1 large onion, sliced and
  sautéed in ¾ cup oil or
  shortening

In a preheated large heavy-bottomed pot over medium heat, combine kasha, egg, salt, and garlic powder stirring constantly until grains are separated./ Add briskly boiling water to pot, cover tightly, and cook approximately 15 minutes./ Add cooked bow ties and browned onion to kasha mixture./ Adjust seasoning to taste, and add shortening if mixture is too dry./

Noodle Kugel (Pudding)

Serves 8

1 lb. broad noodles
Salt
Water
¼ cup oil
4 eggs
¾ cup sugar
½ tsp. cinnamon
1-9 oz. can crushed
  pineapple
Raisins

Cook noodles in boiling salted water until tender./ Drain noodles and toss with oil./ Mix eggs, sugar, ½ teaspoon salt, cinnamon, pineapple, and raisins to taste in a small bowl./ Add mixture to noodles./

Place mixture in a well greased 9 by 14 inch shallow casserole./ In a 350°F. oven bake Kugel for 45 minutes to one hour./ (Kugel is best when made a day in advance, cooled and cut into portions, and reheated before serving.)/

Italian Macaroni And Cheese

Serves 6 to 8

2 lbs. raw spinach
3 to 4 cups marinara sauce
1 lb. ricotta cheese
⅔ cup Parmesan cheese,
  grated
⅓ cup parsley, chopped
3 eggs, lightly beaten
2 tsp. salt
½ tsp. freshly ground pepper
1 lb. tubelike pasta—elbow
  macaroni, etc.

Pick over spinach, discarding tough stems, rinse well and drain./ In a tightly covered saucepan, cook spinach briefly in the water that clings to the leaves./ Drain and let cool./ Press spinach between hands to further remove moisture, then chop.

Combine spinach, marinara sauce, ricotta cheese, Parmesan cheese, parsley, eggs, salt and pepper and blend well./ In a large saucepan, bring salted water to a boil and add pasta, stirring rapidly, and cook for 2 minutes./ Drain in colander. Add pasta to spinach mixture and turn into baking dish./ In a 350°F. oven, bake for 25 to 30 minutes, or until pasta is tender but not mushy./ Do not overcook./ Serve with extra grated Parmesan cheese./

Linguine A La Victor

Serves 4

½ lb. linguine, cooked al
  dente
1 package frozen
  broccoli, parboiled and cut
  in ½" pieces
4 oz. stuffed green olives
3 oz. salad oil
2 sprigs parsley, chopped
  fine
1 tsp. oregano
¼ cup Parmesan cheese,
  grated
2 tbls. butter

In a greased 2 quart casserole, mix together linguine, broccoli, olives, oil, parsley and oregano./ Sprinkle top with Parmesan cheese and dot with butter./ In a 350° F. oven, bake for 25 minutes or until casserole is lightly browned./

Chef: Victor Tremblay   *Brickman Hotel*

Noodle And Cheese Pudding

Serves 6 to 8

½ cup sugar
2 tbls. shortening
4 eggs, separated
1 cup sour cream
¾ cup pot cheese (or cottage
  cheese)
1½ tsp. vanilla
1-8 oz. package medium egg
  noodles, parboiled
½ tsp. salt

Cream together sugar and shortening./ Beat egg yolks and add to creamed mixture./ Add sour cream, pot cheese, and vanilla./ Blend mixture with parboiled noodles, and add salt./ Fold stiffly beaten egg whites into mixture./ Turn noodle pudding into greased casserole dish and bake in pan of hot water in a 300°F. oven approximately one hour./

Lasagna a La Catskills

Serves 6

3 tbls. butter or margarine
1 lb. lean ground chuck
2-8 oz. cans tomato sauce
1 cup sour cream
1-8 oz. package cream
  cheese, softened
⅓ cup scallions, shredded
¼ cup cottage cheese
1 tbls. green pepper, minced
4 cups medium noodles,
  cooked

In a skillet, in one tablespoon butter or margarine, saute ground meat until browned./ Stir in tomato sauce and remove from heat./ In a large bowl, combine sour cream, cream cheese, scallions, cottage cheese and green pepper./ Spread half of cooked noodles in a 2 quart casserole and cover with cheese mixture./ Top with remainder of noodles./ Melt 2 tablespoons butter or margarine and pour over noodles./ Cover with meat and tomato sauce mixture./ (At this point, casserole may be refrigerated until just before serving time for improved flavor or baked immediately.)/ In a 375° F. oven, bake for approximately 45 minutes or until heated through./ Let lasagna rest for 15 minutes before serving./

Lukshen Kugel

Serves 8 to 10

½ lb. broad noodles, cooked
1 lb. creamed cottage cheese
1 cup sour cream
1 cup milk
1-8 oz. can crushed
  pineapple
3 eggs, beaten
¼ cup sugar
¼ cup butter, melted
¼ cup raisins
1 tsp. vanilla
1 tsp. cinnamon
¼ tsp. salt

In a large bowl, stir all ingredients together./ Turn into a well-buttered baking dish./ In a 350°F. oven, bake kugel for one hour, or until top is golden./

Barley And Mushroom Pilaf

Serves 8

4 to 5 tbls. butter
½ lb. mushrooms, sliced
2 medium onions, coarsely
  chopped
1½ cups large pearl barley
3 cups beef (or chicken)
  broth

Melt butter in a saucepan, and sauté mushrooms and onions until soft./ Add barley, and stir over medium-high heat until lightly browned./

In a separate pan, bring broth to a boil./ Pour broth over barley, cover saucepan tightly, reduce heat, and simmer for 45 to 50 minutes./ Pilaf is ready when liquid is absorbed and barley is tender but not mushy./

Green Rice

Serves 12

2 cups brown rice
6 cups water
2 stalks celery, diced
1 medium onion, diced
3 scallions, diced
½ bunch parsley, chopped
½ bunch dill, chopped
2 cloves garlic, diced
Vegetable Bouillon Powder

In a covered saucepan, cook brown rice in boiling water for 15 minutes./ Add celery, onion, scallions, parsley, dill, and garlic./ Continue cooking until all moisture is absorbed./ Season green rice with vegetable bouillon powder./

Vegetarian Hotel

Vegetables

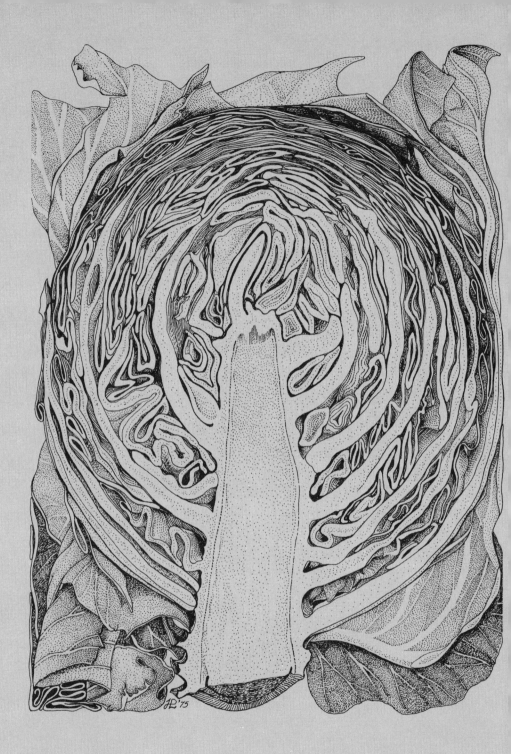

Eggplant And Rice Provencale   *Serves 8 to 10*

2 large eggplants
4 tbls. olive oil
3 cups onion, chopped finely
1 green pepper, cored,
  seeded and cut into 1 inch
  squares
2 cloves garlic, minced finely
½ tsp. thyme
1 bay leaf
3½ cups chicken broth
3 tomatoes, peeled and
  chopped
1 cup raw rice
Salt
Pepper
½ cup grated Parmesan
  cheese

Wash eggplants and pat dry./ Trim ends off and cut eggplant into one inch cubes./ Heat oil in a large (5 to 6 quart) ovenware pot that can be used on top of the stove./ Add eggplant to the pot and cook over high heat, shaking the pot frequently and stirring until all cubes are coated with oil./

Add onion, green pepper, garlic, thyme, bay leaf and eggplant./ Stir in tomatoes and lower heat./ Simmer for 5 minutes until most of the liquid has evaporated and the mixture has thickened./ Stir in chicken broth and rice./ Season mixture with salt and pepper to taste./ Cover pot and cook, stirring occasionally until the rice has absorbed the liquid./ Sprinkle mixture with grated cheese./ Bake in a 400°F. oven for 15 minutes./

Eggplant Souffle   *Serves 6 to 8*

½ cup butter
2 medium eggplants, peeled
  and diced
2 medium onions, diced
½ lb. mushrooms, diced
½ cup matzo meal
2 tbls. grated Parmesan
  cheese
2 tsp. salt
Pepper
6 eggs
1 cup milk
1 lb. mozzarella cheese,
  sliced

Heat butter in skillet./ Sauté eggplant, onion and mushrooms in butter until tender./ Remove skillet from heat and cool./ Add matzo meal, grated cheese, salt and pepper to taste./ Beat eggs and milk together, and add to vegetables./ Mix ingredients well./

Place mixture in greased baking pan or casserole./ Bake souffle in a 350° F. oven for 45 minutes./ Lay mozzarella slices on top and bake an additional 15 minutes or until cheese melts./

Chef: Harry Foo   *Raleigh Hotel*

Green Bean Dish   *Serves 6 to 8*

2 packages frozen green
  beans
1 can mushroom soup
1 can fried onion rings
1-16 oz. can Chinese
  vegetables

Cook green beans as directed on package, and drain./ Place beans on bottom of flat casserole./ Pour mushroom soup evenly over beans./ Mix half the onion rings with Chinese vegetables and pour over mushroom soup./ Top with remaining onion rings./ Bake casserole in a moderate (350° F.) oven for 20 minutes./

Potato Kugel

Serves 4 to 6

2 cups raw potatoes, peeled,
  grated and drained
1 large onion, grated
1 large carrot, grated
2 eggs, beaten
¼ cup flour
¼ cup matzo meal
1½ tsp. salt
1 tsp. baking powder
Pepper
4 tbls. chicken fat

In a bowl, mix together well potatoes, onion, carrot, eggs, flour, matzo meal, baking powder, salt, pepper to taste and 2 tablespoons chicken fat./ Place mixture in a greased baking dish and pour remaining chicken fat on top./ In a 375° F. oven, bake kugel one to 1½ hours, or until top is crisp and brown./

Irish Colcannon

Serves 4 to 6

1 small head green cabbage,
  shredded
1 cup water
4 large potatoes, peeled,
  cooked and mashed
½ cup scallions, chopped
  finely
¼ to ½ cup milk (or cream)
6 tbls. butter (or margarine)
1 tsp. salt
Ground pepper

In a covered saucepan, cook cabbage in boiling water until cabbage is crisp tender./ Drain cabbage well./ Blend cabbage with hot mashed potatoes and milk, beating well./ Mix in scallions, 4 tablespoons butter, salt and pepper to taste./ Spoon mixture into ovenproof casserole and dot with 2 tablespoons butter./ Place casserole 6 inches under broiler and broil until it is bubbly and golden./

Broccoli Au Gratin

Serves 8 to 10

6 tbls. butter
6 tbls. flour
1½ tsp. salt
¼ tsp. dry mustard
2¾ cups milk
¾ cup cheddar cheese,
  diced
4 packages frozen
  chopped broccoli,
  cooked and drained
Grated Parmesan cheese
Paprika
Slivered almonds

Melt butter in saucepan./ Add flour, salt, and mustard and cook until mixture bubbles./ Gradually add milk, stirring until mixture is thick and smooth./ Add diced cheddar cheese, stirring until it melts./ Add broccoli./

Pour broccoli mixture into greased casserole, and sprinkle with Parmesan cheese, paprika, and almonds./ In a 350° F. oven, bake casserole for approximately ½ hour, or until hot and bubbling./

Casserole can be prepared in advance, and stored in refrigerator or frozen./ Add topping only before heating./

Vegetable Medley, Chinese-Style

Serves 4

1 tbls. shortening
3 cups cabbage, shredded
1 cup celery, cut in thin
  diagonal pieces
1 medium green pepper, cut
  in thin diagonal pieces
⅔ cup onion, chopped
1 tsp. salt
⅛ tsp. pepper
1 tbls. soy sauce

Heat shortening in a medium-sized skillet./ Add cabbage, celery, pepper, and onion to skillet, and stir./ Cover skillet and steam vegetables 5 minutes or until they are crisp and tender, stirring several times./ Add salt, pepper, and soy sauce, if desired./ Stir medley again./

Banana And Eggplant

Serves 4 to 6

2 tbls. olive oil
1 medium eggplant, peeled
  and cubed
1 medium onion, sliced
3 bananas, sliced
1-15 oz. can tomato sauce
2 tsp. marjoram
Salt
Pepper

Heat oil in a skillet./ Fry eggplant and onions in oil until golden./ Add bananas, tomato sauce, marjoram, salt and pepper to taste./ Simmer mixture until eggplant is soft./

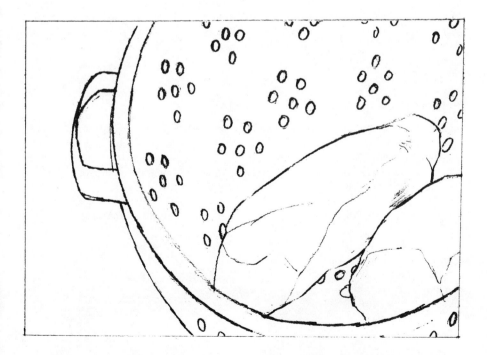

Fontana Espana

Serves 2 to 3

3 tbls. olive oil
2 small cloves garlic, minced
1 medium zucchini, cut into
  ¼ inch slices
½ eggplant, cut into ¼ inch
  slices
½ green pepper, cut into
  1 inch squares
½ red pepper, cut into
  1 inch squares
½ medium tomato, diced
8 medium mushrooms, sliced
½ cup tomato sauce
2 large slices Monterey Jack
  cheese (or mozzarella
  cheese)

In a large saucepan or Dutch oven, heat oil and sauté garlic until it is brown./ Add zucchini, eggplant, green pepper, red pepper, tomato and mushrooms./ Cook over high heat, stirring constantly to prevent burning./ When all vegetables start browning, add tomato sauce./ Stir well for approximately one minute./

Remove mixture to ovenproof casserole./ Place cheese on top./ Brown cheese under broiler or in hot oven./ Serve casserole with steaming rice or pasta./

Paul's Potpourri Restaurant

Potato Latkes

Serves 4 to 6

4-5 raw potatoes, peeled and
  grated
1 medium onion, grated
2 eggs
¼ cup matzo meal
Salt
Pepper
Peanut oil

In a bowl, combine potatoes, onion, eggs, matzo meal and salt and pepper to taste./ In a large heavy skillet, heat oil to depth of ½ inch./ Drop potato mixture by tablespoons into hot oil and fry over high heat until browned on one side./ Turn and brown other side./ Drain on absorbent paper./

Kaplan's Delicatessen

Fritadu De Espinaca (Spinach Souffle)

Serves 10

12 cups fresh spinach,
  chopped very finely
8 eggs, yolks and whites
  beaten separately
8 oz. small curd cottage
  cheese
4 oz. grated Parmesan
  cheese
2 medium potatoes, boiled
  and grated (or ¼ cup
  potato flakes)
1½ tsp. salt
Oil

In a large bowl, thoroughly mix spinach, beaten egg yolks, both cheeses, potato, and salt./ Fold in egg whites, beaten until stiff./ Pour oil in bottom of baking pan and heat it in oven./ When oil is hot, pour spinach mixture in baking pan and bake in a 350° F. oven for approximately one hour, or until souffle is golden brown and firm./

Allow souffle to cool slightly, and then cut it into serving squares./

Souffle can be frozen and reheated in a 350° F. oven for serving./

Garden Souffle

Serves 8

3 lbs. spinach
1 cup water
4 medium zucchini,
  unpeeled and sliced ¼ inch
  thick
¼ cup olive oil
3 tbls. Parmesan cheese,
  grated
4 eggs
2 slices bread, crust removed
¼ cup light cream
¼ cup parsley, chopped
⅛ tsp. pepper
Thyme
Salt
3 green onions, sliced

Wash spinach thoroughly and drain./ In a saucepan, steam spinach in water for 5 minutes, then drain again and chop finely./ In a covered frying pan, sauté zucchini in oil, steaming it lightly—do not cook it thoroughly./ Add cheese to spinach./ Add eggs, one at a time, beating well after each addition./ Soak the bread slices in the cream and whip into spinach mixture./ Add parsley, pepper, a pinch of thyme and salt to taste./ Fold in zucchini and green onions, taking care to leave squash slices whole./ In a greased 12 by 8 by 2 inch baking dish, in a 350° F. oven, bake souffle for approximately 45 minutes, or until a toothpick inserted in the center comes out clean./

Broccoli With Bamboo Shoots

Serves 4

¼ cup vegetable oil
2 cloves garlic, crushed
1 lb. fresh broccoli, cleaned
  and cut in ½ inch thick
  spears
½ cup bamboo shoots
¼ cup chicken broth
2 tbls. soy sauce
½ tsp. salt
¼ tsp. pepper

Heat oil in a skillet, and stir in garlic./ Add broccoli and toss it until it is well coated./ Add bamboo shoots, broth, soy sauce, salt and pepper./ (Adjust salt and pepper quantities to taste)./ Simmer broccoli in the uncovered skillet 25 minutes, or until it is tender./ Stir occasionally./

Potato-Cheese Bake

Serves 6

½ cup onion, chopped
2 tbls. butter
3 cups raw potatoes, peeled
  and grated
1 cup sharp Cheddar cheese,
  grated
2 eggs, beaten
1½ tsp. salt
1 tsp. paprika
⅛ tsp. pepper
2 slices white bread

In a frying pan, sauté the chopped onion in butter until soft./ Mix in the potatoes, cheese, eggs, salt, paprika and pepper./ Soak bread in water to cover until soft, squeeze dry and add to potato mixture, mixing well./ Turn mixture into a buttered one quart casserole./ In a 350° F. oven bake for one hour./

Vegetable Casserole

Serves 8 to 10

1 cup fresh cauliflower, cut
in small pieces
1 cup fresh green beans, cut
1 cup fresh peas
1 cup fresh zucchini, sliced
or diced
1 cup onions, diced
1 cup green peppers, diced
1 cup eggplant, peeled and
diced
1 cup fresh broccoli, diced
1 quart crushed tomatoes
¼ cup vinegar
¼ cup honey
1 tsp. basil
1 tsp. oregano
¼ cup toasted wheat germ
¼ cup cashew nuts, ground

Choose from the eight listed vegetables, in any desired combination, sufficient vegetables to fill a 1½ to 2 quart baking dish./ Mix well crushed tomatoes, vinegar, honey, basil, and oregano to make tomato sauce./ Cover vegetables with sauce./ If sauce is too thick, add some water so vegetables will have sufficient liquid for cooking./ Top mixture with wheat germ mixed with cashews./ Bake casserole in 350° F. oven for one hour./

Eggplant Supreme

Serves 4 to 6

1 medium eggplant
2 medium onions
Water
Salt
½ cup margarine
½ cup matzo meal
1 egg, lightly beaten
Pepper

Peel and dice eggplant./ Cut up one onion and boil it in a saucepan with eggplant, water, and a little salt./ In a frying pan, melt margarine./ Dice remaining onion and brown it in frying pan./ Add matzo meal to browned onion and remove pan from heat./

Drain most of the water from boiled eggplant./ Mash eggplant in mixing bowl./ Add beaten egg and half the mixture from the frying pan./ Add salt and pepper to taste./ Place mixture in baking dish./ Put the rest of the matzo meal mixture on top./ Bake in a 350° F. oven for ½ hour./

Eggplant Steak

Serves 4

1 medium eggplant
2 tbls. vegetable oil
6 tbls. raw wheat germ
Garlic powder
Vegetable Bouillon Powder

Slice eggplant into ¾ inch wide slices./ Oil baking pan./ Dip eggplant slices in oil on one side, and place slices in pan oiled side up./ Cover slices with raw wheat germ, and sprinkle them lightly with garlic powder./ In a preheated 350° F. oven, bake eggplant steak for 45 minutes./ Season dish with vegetable bouillon powder./

Vegetarian Hotel

Brussels Sprouts Parisienne

Serves 6 to 8

1½ lbs. fresh brussel sprouts
(or 2 packages, frozen)
Water, salted
2 tbls. butter
2 tbls. flour
½ tsp. salt
⅛ tsp. nutmeg
Pepper
1-10½ oz. can chicken
broth
2 egg yolks, beaten
¼ cup toasted almonds

Wash sprouts thoroughly, and trim off stem ends./ Place sprouts in an uncovered saucepan with salted water to cover./ Cook them approximately 7 to 10 minutes, until tender and crisp./ Drain sprouts./

In a large saucepan, melt butter and blend in flour, salt, nutmeg, and a dash of pepper./ Cook mixture over low heat until it is smooth and bubbly./ Remove pan from heat, and stir in chicken broth./ Return pan to burner, and bring mixture to boil, stirring./ Reduce heat and simmer one minute./

Slowly stir half the hot sauce into the beaten egg yolks./ Pour egg yolk mixture back into saucepan./ Boil it one additional minute, stirring constantly./ Stir in toasted almonds and sprouts, and heat them thoroughly./

Beet Casserole A La Russe

Serves 6 to 8

12 medium beets, well-
scrubbed
½ cup sour cream
½ medium green pepper,
minced
1 tbls. lemon juice
½ tsp. salt
Garlic
Buttered fresh bread crumbs

In a saucepan, boil beets approximately 45 minutes, or until tender./ Press beets through ricer./ Combine sour cream, green pepper, lemon juice and salt and add to beets./ Rub a casserole with garlic and turn beet mixture into it./ Cover with bread crumbs./ In a 350° F. oven, bake for 20 minutes./ (If desired, this dish may be prepared in advance and reheated before serving.)/

"Swiftly Spiced" Sweet Potatoes

Serves 8 to 10

3 lbs. sweet potatoes
Boiling water, salted
12 tbls. light brown sugar,
packed
3 tbls. butter
½ tsp. cinnamon
½ tsp. nutmeg
¼ tsp. salt
1 cup milk

In a large saucepan, cook sweet potatoes in boiling water until potatoes are tender./ Peel potatoes and mash them./ Stir into mashed potatoes 10 tbls. sugar, butter, cinnamon, nutmeg, salt and milk./

Turn mixture into greased 1½ quart casserole and sprinkle mixture with 2 tablespoons sugar./ Bake casserole in a preheated 400° F. oven for 30 minutes./

Vegetable Chow Mein

Serves 6

2 tbls. oil
2 cups Chinese cabbage
1½ cups celery, sliced
1 cup onions, sliced
1 cup mushrooms, sliced
1 cup green pepper, seeded
   and cut into strips
1 cup beansprouts
¾ cup water chestnuts,
   thinly sliced
¾ cup bamboo shoots
2 cups water
3 tbls. soy sauce
1½ tbls. cornstarch
½ cup scallions, minced
Chow Mein noodles
Boiled white rice

In a saucepan, heat oil and quickly sauté all vegetables for 3 minutes./ Add one cup of water and soy sauce and continue cooking for 5 minutes./ Mix cornstarch with remaining one cup water and add to mixture, stirring until thickened./ Add scallions./ Crisp noodles in oven and arrange on platter./ Turn chow mein out on top of noodles./ Serve with rice./

Grossinger Hotel

Lima Bean Casserole

Serves 4 to 6

1 lb. large dried lima beans,
   washed
6 cups water
¼ lb. salt pork
1 medium onion, sliced thin
½ cup dark molasses
½ cup chili sauce
2 tbls. brown sugar
1 tbls. vinegar
2 tsp. salt
1 tsp. dry mustard
½ cup maple syrup

In a large saucepan, cover beans with water and let stand overnight./ The next morning, pour beans and water into a large kettle, adding enough water to cover beans./ Bring kettle to a boil, cover and simmer for ½ hour./ Drain beans, reserving liquid, and place beans in a 2 quart casserole./
Cut salt pork in half, grind one half and cut the other half into small squares./ Add onion, molasses, chili sauce, brown sugar, vinegar, salt and dry mustard to casserole and mix well with beans./ Top with ground and diced salt pork./ In a 300°F. oven, bake 2 hours./ Stir maple syrup into casserole and continue baking approximately ½ hour more./ (if casserole starts to dry out during baking, add reserved bean liquid as needed.)/

Salads and
Salad Dressings

Oriental Cabbage Slaw

Serves 8 to 10

¾ cup mayonnaise
2 tbls. soy sauce
2 tsp. sugar
1 tsp. salt
1 medium head cabbage,
  shredded (about 8 cups)
½ cup green onions,
  chopped
1-6 oz. or 8½ oz. can water
  chestnuts, drained and
  thinly sliced
1-5 oz. or 6 oz. can bamboo
  shoots, drained and diced

In large bowl, mix with fork, mayonnaise, soy sauce, sugar, and salt./ Add cabbage, onions, water chestnuts, and bamboo shoots./ Toss slaw until cabbage mixture is well coated./

Apple Cole Slaw

Yield: 6 cups

3 cups McIntosh apples,
  peeled, cored and diced
2 tbls. lemon juice
3 cups white cabbage, finely
  shredded
1 cup Swiss cheese, diced
⅔ cup walnuts, chopped
1 tsp. salt
¼ tsp. pepper
⅔ cup mayonnaise
½ cup sour cream
2 tsp. sugar

In a bowl, toss apples with lemon juice./ Add cabbage, cheese, walnuts, salt and pepper./ In a separate bowl, combine mayonnaise, sour cream and sugar./ Pour dressing over the slaw./ Toss well and season with salt and pepper to taste./ Chill for at least 4 hours before serving./

Poor People's Salad

Serves 8 to 10

1-16 oz. can string beans
1-16 oz. can kidney beans
1-16 oz. can lima beans
1-16 oz. can navy beans
1 cup onion, chopped
½ cup wine (or cider)
  vinegar
½ cup water
¼ cup olive oil
¼ cup vegetable oil
Salt
Pepper

Rinse all beans carefully under running water./ Mix beans, onion, vinegar, water, oils, and salt and pepper to taste./ Add more water or vinegar to taste./ Refrigerate salad until serving./

Happy Vineyard Restaurant

French Dressing

Yield: 2½ cups

1½ cups olive oil (½ may
  be peanut oil)
¾ cup tarragon vinegar
½ cup sugar
1 tsp. salt
¾ tsp. grated onion (or
  onion juice)
½ tsp. curry powder
¼ tsp. pepper
Cayenne
1 clove garlic, peeled and
  left whole

In a bowl, mix oil, vinegar, sugar, salt, onion, curry powder, pepper and a dash of cayenne together with egg beater./ Add garlic clove and pour into Mason jar./ Let dressing stand 24 hours before using, then shake well each time./

Cucumber Salad

Serves 6

1 cup water
1-3 oz. package lemon-
  flavored gelatin
1 cup small curd cottage
  cheese
1 cup cucumber, chopped
  finely and drained
½ cup mayonnaise
¼ cup chopped nuts
1 tbls. pimento, chopped
1 tsp. onion, minced
½ tsp. salt
⅛ tsp. white pepper

Dissolve gelatin in boiling water; then let it cool./ Add cottage cheese to gelatin, and beat well with rotary beater./ Add cucumber, mayonnaise, nuts, pimento, onion, salt, and pepper./ Blend ingredients thoroughly./ Grease well 6 individual molds, and pour in blended mixture./ Place molds in refrigerator until set./

To serve, unmold salad on several lettuce leaves, and decorate it with pimento./

Drue's Dutch Potato Salad

Serves 8

6 to 8 medium potatoes
2 stalks celery, diced
1 large onion, diced
4 to 5 strips bacon, fried and
  crumbled, reserve fat
4 eggs, hard boiled, sliced
1 cup sugar
1 cup vinegar
1 cup water
4 to 6 raw eggs, beaten
1 tsp. dry mustard
½ tsp. celery seeds
  (optional)

Boil potatoes in their jackets, peel and slice while they are still hot./ Combine potatoes, celery, onion, bacon, and hard boiled eggs in bowl./

In a saucepan, combine bacon fat, sugar, vinegar, water, beaten eggs, dry mustard, and celery seeds, if desired./ Cook for 15 minutes, stirring constantly./ Pour over potato mixture in bowl.

Potato salad is best made the day it is to be used, and not refrigerated.

Calhoun's Catering

Shrimp Salad

Serves 6

1 lb. shrimp, cooked, shelled,
    and deveined
4 eggs, hard-boiled, cut into
    bite-sized pieces
½ cup celery, chopped
½ cup cucumber, cubed
⅓ cup pitted, black olives,
    sliced
¼ cup pecan bits
1 tsp. sweet relish
½ tsp. garlic powder
1 small onion, grated
Salt
Pepper
Mayonnaise

Cut shrimp into bite-sized pieces, and place them in a bowl./ Add eggs, celery, cucumber, olives, pecans, relish, garlic powder, onion, and salt and pepper to taste./ Mix ingredients, adding enough mayonnaise to bind./

Refrigerate 2 to 4 hours before serving./ Serve salad on lettuce leaves with tomato slices./ Garnish with olives, cucumbers, radish roses, etc./ Chicken cut into bite-sized pieces may be substituted for shrimp./ Garnish chicken salad with drained pineapple chunks./

Wilted Salad

Serves 8

3 slices bacon
½ cup vinegar
2 tsp. sugar
½ tsp. dry mustard
½ tsp. salt
Black pepper, freshly ground
1 head leaf lettuce
1 tbls. chives, chopped
2 eggs, hard boiled and sliced
1 sprig dill

In a small skillet, cook bacon until crisp./ Drain bacon, crumble, and set aside, reserving fat in skillet./ Add to the bacon fat vinegar, sugar, mustard, salt, and pepper to taste./ Simmer mixture approximately 2 minutes./

Wash lettuce, tear into pieces, and place in salad bowl./ Pour mixture from skillet over lettuce./ Add crumbled bacon, chives, eggs, and dill./ Toss salad and serve at once./

Garlic Salad Dressing

Yield: 1 quart

4 eggs
3 cloves garlic, finely
    chopped
1 tsp. salt
1 tsp. sugar
½ tsp. pepper, freshly
    ground
3 cups oil
1 cup vinegar

With an electric mixer, beat eggs in mixing bowl for approximately ½ hour, or until very thick and white./ Beat in garlic, salt, sugar and pepper./ Gradually add oil and vinegar, beating until smooth./

Steak Pub Restaurant

Spinach Salad

Serves 8

1 bag fresh spinach, cleaned,
  picked over, dried, and torn
  into small pieces
½ large, red onion, sliced
  into thin rings
⅓ lb. fresh mushrooms,
  sliced thinly
2 tbls. lemon juice
2 eggs, hard boiled, chopped
½ lb. bacon, fried and
  crumbled
⅓ cup vegetable oil
1½ tbls. wine vinegar
½ tsp. dry mustard
⅓ tsp. garlic powder
Salt
Black pepper, freshly ground

Place spinach in large bowl./ Add sliced onion and mushrooms./ Sprinkle lemon juice on top, tossing to coat all mushrooms with juice./ Add eggs, bacon, oil, vinegar, mustard, garlic powder, dash of salt, and pepper to taste, and mix well./

Sauerkraut Salad

Serves 12

2 cups sugar
1 cup vinegar
2 lbs. canned (or bagged)
  sauerkraut
1 lb. canned bean sprouts
2 cups celery, chopped
2 cups onion, chopped
½ cup red and green
  peppers, diced
2 tsp. whole celery seed
½ tsp. oregano
Salt

In a saucepan, mix sugar and vinegar, and bring to full boil./ Let mixture cool 15 minutes./ Combine vinegar mixture with sauerkraut, bean sprouts, celery, onion, pepper, celery seed, oregano, and salt to taste./ Mix well./

Store sauerkraut salad in covered glass or plastic container in refrigerator./ It will keep two months./

Egg Salad

Serves 4

2 tbls. onion, chopped finely
6 hard boiled eggs
1 stalk celery, diced
⅓ cup mayonnaise
1 heaping tbls. prepared
  mustard
½ tsp. salt
¼ tsp. pepper
¼ tsp. curry powder

In chopping bowl, add eggs to minced onion and mash them together./ Add celery, mayonnaise, mustard, salt, pepper, and curry powder./ Blend ingredients well./ Adjust salt and pepper to taste./

Horseradish Mold

Serves: 4 to 6

1-3 oz. package lemon
  gelatin
¾ cup hot water
¾ cup beet juice
1 cup beets, diced
1 stalk celery, diced
1 tbls. prepared red
  horseradish
1 tbls. lemon juice
1 tsp. onion juice

In a bowl, dissolve gelatin in hot water./ Stir in beet juice and place in refrigerator until partially set./ Mix beets, celery, horseradish, lemon juice and onion juice into gelatin and pour into lightly greased mold./ Refrigerate until set./

Super Seafood Salad

Serves 6 to 8

1 head Romaine lettuce
½ lb. spinach
1 zucchini, sliced
3 scallions, sliced
12 black olives, pitted
12 stuffed green olives,
  (with pimento)
2 slices Swiss cheese, diced
2 tomatoes, quartered
5 marinated artichoke hearts,
  halved
1 lb. seafood (crabmeat,
  shrimp, lobster, tunafish,
  or flaked fresh fish, or
  combination of these)
Croutons
Bottled Caesar dressing

Wash lettuce and spinach, tear them in pieces, and place in large salad bowl./ Add zucchini, scallions, black and green olives as desired, and diced cheese./ Place tomato and artichoke wedges around the bowl./ Put all the seafood in the middle of the bowl, and place croutons on top./ Add dressing and toss salad./

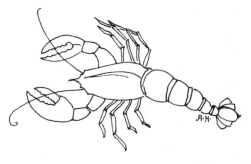

Burgundy Cranberry Relish

Yield: 8 to 12

1-6 oz. package raspberry
  gelatin
2 cups boiling water
1-16 oz. can whole
  cranberry sauce
1-8¾ oz. can crushed
  pineapple
½ cup Burgundy wine
⅓ cup chopped walnuts

Dissolve gelatin in boiling water./ Stir cranberry sauce, undrained pineapple, and wine into gelatin./ Chill until partially set./ Stir nuts into mixture, pour into a 6 cup mold, and chill relish until firm./

Cranberry Orange Relish Mold

Serves 8 to 10

1-28 oz. can pineapple slices
1-9 oz. can (1 cup) crushed
 pineapple
1-3 oz. package cherry-
 flavored gelatin
¼ cup sugar
1 tbls. lemon juice
1-16 oz. can whole berry
 cranberry sauce
1 small unpared orange or
 tangerine, quartered,
 seeded and cut into small
 pieces
½ cup walnuts, broken

Drain both kinds of pineapple and reserve syrup./ In a saucepan, combine gelatin and sugar./ Add enough water to reserved syrup to equal 2 cups, then add liquid to gelatin mixture./ Heat and stir over low heat until gelatin and sugar dissolve./ Add lemon juice./ Chill until partially set./

In a blender, grind orange pieces using a few spoonfuls of cranberry sauce as an aid in even grinding./ Add ground fruit, remainder of cranberry sauce, crushed pineapple and nuts to gelatin mixture./ Pour into greased mold and chill until firm./ Unmold onto pineapple slices on platter for serving./

Dandelion Salad With Italian Dressing

Serves 6

1 lb. dandelion greens
1 medium onion, diced
1 pimento, minced
½ cup cider vinegar
½ cup water
½ cup olive oil
½ tsp. sugar
½ tsp. salt
⅛ tsp. pepper
⅛ tsp. oregano
Whites of 2 hard-boiled eggs,
 riced

Remove flowers and stems from dandelion greens, wash them thoroughly and cut into 2 inch pieces./ In a salad bowl, combine greens, onion and pimento./ In another bowl, mix together vinegar, water, oil, sugar, salt, pepper and oregano./ Pour dressing over greens and toss./ Sprinkle egg whites over top of salad./ (As a variation, sauté diced bacon in skillet, then add all dressing ingredients except olive oil, bring to boil and pour over salad.)/

Breads

Pumpkin Bread

Yield: 4 loaves

4 eggs
2½ cups sugar
1 cup vegetable oil
3 ½ cups flour
2 tsp. baking soda
1 tsp. cinnamon
¾ tsp. salt
1 lb. can pumpkin
1 cup chopped walnuts

Beat eggs, sugar, and oil together./ Mix flour with baking soda, cinnamon, and salt./ Slowly add flour and pumpkin, alternately, to egg mixture, mixing well after each addition./ Stir walnuts into batter./

Grease and flour 4 one-pound coffee cans./ Fill each can half full with batter, and bake in a 350° F. oven for one hour./ (Bread may be wrapped in a foil or plastic wrap, and placed in can for mailing.)/

Buttermilk Biscuits

Yield: 9 to 12 biscuits

1 cup thick buttermilk, warm
¼ cup and 1 tsp. sugar
3 tbls. oil
1 tsp. salt
¼ tsp. baking soda
1 package yeast
¼ cup warm water
2½ to 2¾ cups sifted flour

Mix together buttermilk, ¼ cup sugar, oil, salt, and baking soda./ Dissolve yeast in water with one teaspoon sugar, and add to buttermilk mixture./ In two additions, mix flour in, using just enough flour to make dough easy to handle./ Turn out on floured board, and knead a few turns./ Cut dough into 9 to 12 pieces./ Roll pieces by hand to make balls./

Place balls on a well greased sheet./ Let them rise until doubled in volume./ In a 400° F. oven, bake for 25 to 30 minutes, on until done to taste./

Oatmeal Bread

Yield: 2 loaves

2 cups oatmeal, regular or
    quick
2 tbls. shortening
2½ cups water
2 packages dry yeast
½ cup brown sugar
2 tsp. salt
Flour
Sugar water (or shortening
    melted)

Combine oatmeal and shortening./ Pour two cups boiling water over oatmeal, stir, and let cool until lukewarm./ Dissolve yeast in ½ cup lukewarm water, and add to oatmeal mixture./ Add brown sugar, salt, and enough flour to form soft dough./ Knead dough./ Cover bowl with cloth and let it rise, then punch it down./

Place dough in 2 greased loaf pans and allow it to rise again./ In a 375°F. oven, bake bread for 35 to 40 minutes./ Turn loaves out on sides./ Brush top of bread with sugar water or melted shortening./

Speedy Pumpernickel Loaf

Yield: 1 loaf

1 package (13¾ oz.) hot roll
  mix
2 eggs, separated
¾ cup warm water
¼ cup molasses
¾ cup rye flour, unsifted
1½ tsp. caraway seed

Prepare hot roll mix as directed on package, using one whole egg and one egg yolk./ Reserve egg white./ Pour warm water into a bowl and stir in molasses./ Add rye flour, prepared roll mix and caraway seeds, stirring./ Place dough in a greased bowl, lightly grease top of dough, cover bowl with cloth and let dough rise in a warm, draft-free place for approximately 45 minutes./ Punch dough down./ Turn out on floured board and shape into a ball./ Place on a buttered baking sheet, cover, and let rise again approximately 45 minutes./ Brush lightly with beaten egg white and sprinkle with additional caraway seeds./ In a 375° F. oven, bake pumpernickel loaf for 35 to 40 minutes./

Potato Drop Biscuit

Yield: 36 biscuits

2 cups potatoes, boiled,
  peeled and mashed
½ yeast cake, dissolve in 2
  tbls. warm water
½ cup milk, lukewarm
2 tbls. sugar
2 tbls. shortening, melted
1 tsp. salt
2 cups flour
1 egg, beaten

Combine mashed potatoes, yeast, milk, sugar, shortening and salt./ Add enough flour to make a soft dough./ Let dough rise 2 hours./ Add egg and remaining flour to dough, and mix with wooden spoon./ Let dough rise./ Drop by tablespoons into a greased muffin pan and let dough rise again./ In a 375° F. oven, bake biscuits for approximately 20 minutes./

Crullers

Yield: 24 biscuits

4 eggs
1½ cups sugar
1¼ cup milk
1 tbls. butter, melted
1 tsp. salt
4 cups flour, sifted
3 tsp. baking powder
Lard or vegetable shortening
Confectioners' sugar

In a bowl, beat eggs until light./ Add sugar, gradually, beating until mixture is creamy and well blended./ Add milk, butter and salt./ Sift together flour and baking powder and add to mixture, mixing well./ Turn out onto well-floured board and add just enough flour so dough can be handled well./ Roll dough ¼ inch thick and cut into strips./ In a skillet, fry dough in deep fat heated to 375° F. until golden brown./ Drain on brown paper./ When slightly cooled, sprinkle crullers with confectioners' sugar./

Zucchini Bread

Yield: 1 loaf

1 cup sugar
½ cup oil
2 eggs
1 tsp. lemon peel, grated
½ tsp. orange extract
1½ cups flour
2 tsp. baking powder
½ tsp. baking soda
½ tsp. salt
⅛ tsp. nutmeg
⅛ tsp. ground ginger
1 cup unpeeled zucchini,
   grated
½ cup nuts

Beat sugar, oil, eggs, lemon peel, and orange extract together./ Sift together flour, baking powder, baking soda, salt, nutmeg, and ginger./ Add flour mixture alternately with zucchini to sugar mixture./ Beat well, and stir in nuts./ Pour batter into greased loaf pan./ In a 375° F. oven, bake zucchini bread 55 minutes./ Cool bread in pan 15 minutes./

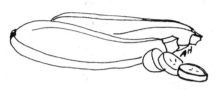

Sour Rye Bread

Yield: 2 loaves

1 cup lukewarm water
1 oz. yeast
1 tbls. sugar
1 cup regular all-purpose
   flour
2 cups buttermilk (or sour
   milk)
2 tbls. caraway seeds
1 tbls. salt
1½ cups whole wheat flour
Approximately 4 cups rye
   flour
Vegetable oil (or melted
   butter)

Dissolve yeast and sugar in lukewarm water./ Blend white flour into mixture and let stand approximately 20 to 25 minutes, or until bubbly and slightly risen./ Warm buttermilk and stir in caraway seed and salt./ Blend buttermilk mixture with yeast sponge./ Stir in whole wheat flour, then enough rye flour to form soft dough./ Knead dough on board lightly floured with rye flour, until smooth and elastic./ Place dough in bowl, grease its top lightly with oil, cover bowl with cloth and let dough rise to double its size./ Punch dough down, then knead it./ Let it rest 5 minutes./ Divide dough in half and shape it into 2 round loaves./ Cover them, and let rise to almost double in size./ Place in pans and bake in 350° F. oven approximately 50 minutes, or until brown./

Ethel's Cottage Cheese Pancakes

Yield: 8 to 10 pancakes

2 eggs
¾ cup sour cream
½ cup sifted flour
⅓ cup cottage cheese
½ tsp. baking soda
½ tsp. salt

Place all ingredients in a blender, cover, and mix until batter is well blended./ (Alternatively, place ingredients in bowl and blend with portable electric mixer.)/ Let batter stand 10 minutes./ Ladle pancakes onto a buttered, hot (400° F.) griddle and cook until brown, turning once./

Ginger Gems

Yield: 12 muffins

½ cup honey
½ cup molasses
1 egg
1½ tbls. butter
½ cup boiling water
Scant ½ tsp. baking soda
1 heaping cup whole wheat
  flour
½ tsp. cinnamon
½ tsp. ginger

Mix honey, molasses, egg, and butter./ Dissolve baking soda in boiling water and add to mixture./ Mix cinnamon and ginger into flour, and stir dry ingredients into liquid mixture./ Bake in greased muffin tins, in a 350° F. oven for 10 to 15 minutes./ Serve ginger gems warm, with butter./

No-Knead Rolls

Yield: 18 rolls

1 cup hot water
6 tbls. shortening
¼ cup sugar
1 tsp. salt
1 package yeast
2 tsp. lukewarm water
3¼ to 4 cups flour
1 egg, well beaten
Milk

In a large bowl, combine hot water, shortening, sugar and salt./ Let mixture cool to lukewarm./ Dissolve yeast in lukewarm water and add to mixture./ Add half the flour and beaten egg and beat well./ Stir in more flour slowly until dough can be easily handled./ Place in a greased bowl, lightly grease top of dough, cover bowl with plastic wrap and refrigerate overnight./

Turn dough out onto lightly floured board and roll to ½ inch thickness./ Cut into 2¼ inch rounds, then form each into a smooth ball./ Place balls on greased cookie sheet, brush with milk, slash tops crosswise and let rise, covered, in a warm place until doubled in volume./ In a 425°F. oven, bake rolls for 12 to 15 minutes./

Beer Waffles

Yield: 16 waffles

3½ cups flour
3 cups light beer
½ cup oil
2 eggs
2 tsp. lemon rind, grated
1 tsp. fresh lemon juice
½ tsp. vanilla
½ tsp. salt

Beat flour, beer, oil, eggs, lemon rind, lemon juice, vanilla, and salt together until smooth./ Let batter stand at least 2 hours to allow rising./ (If batter is to be used next day, cover and store in refrigerator, allowing it to rise before cooking./

Spread batter not too thickly on hot waffle grid./ Check waffles often, as they brown easily./ The beer leaves no taste, but makes waffles light and crisp./ Serve with sour cream and brown sugar, cinnamon sugar, or fruit toppings, or with syrup./

Challah (Egg Bread)

Yield: 2 loaves

½ cup sugar
1 package yeast
1¾ cups warm water
6 cups flour
1 tbls. salt
2 eggs
¼ cup fat (or 2 oz.
  margarine), melted
Oil
Egg Whites
Poppy seeds

Combine sugar, yeast, and ¼ cup warm water; let mixture stand 5 minutes./ Sift together flour and salt./ Place 3 cups of flour in a bowl, make a well in the center and drop the eggs, fat, remaining water, and yeast mixture into it./ Stir and add remaining flour./ Knead dough until it is smooth and elastic./ Place dough in a bowl, and brush top of dough with a little oil./ Cover with a cloth, and let rise 4 to 6 hours, until double in volume./

Divide the dough into 2 equal portions, and set in pans./ Brush dough with egg white, and sprinkle top with poppy seeds./ Let dough rise ½ hour./ Bake in a 400° F. oven for ½ hour or until golden brown./

Health Food Muffins

Yield: 18 to 24 muffins

4 eggs, separated
6 tbls. honey
6 tbls. butter, melted
1 cup sour cream (or yogurt)
1 cup whole wheat flour
1 cup oat flour (or quick-
  cooking oatmeal)
½ cup bran flour
2 tbls. wheat germ
1 tsp. baking soda
½ tsp. vanilla extract
⅛ to ¼ tsp. salt

Cream together egg yolks, honey, and butter./ Add sour cream, whole wheat flour, oat flour, bran flour, and wheat germ, and mix well./ Add baking soda, vanilla, and salt, and mix ingredients again./ Beat egg whites until they are stiff./ Fold egg whites into mixture./

Pour batter into greased or paper lined muffin tins./ In a 325° F. oven bake muffins for approximately 25 minutes./

Dumplings (Hungarian Noodles)

Yield: approximately 100

3 cups sifted flour
2 small eggs
Salt
Water

Beat together flour, eggs, one teaspoon salt, and enough water to make a fairly soft dough./ Form small bits of dough by using the tip of a spoon, cutting dough on a breadboard, or using a spaetzle pan (grinder similar to a Foley mill)./ Quickly drop small bits of dough into boiling salted water./ When dough bits rise to the top, skim them off with a slotted spoon and pile in a hot bowl./

Dumplings can be used whenever macaroni or noodles are called for, and are very good in a casserole with cheese./

Boston Brown Bread

Yield: 1 loaf

1½ cups graham flour
1 cup wheat flour
½ cup sugar
1 tsp. salt
1 tsp. baking soda
½ cup molasses
1 cup sweet milk
1 cup sour milk

In a mixing bowl, combine graham flour, wheat flour, sugar, and salt./ In another bowl, stir baking soda into molasses./ Mix molasses with sweet and sour milk./ Add liquid to dry ingredients and mix well./ If dough is too thin, add more graham flour./ Spread dough in baking pan and bake in a 350° F. oven for one hour./

Ice Box Biscuits

Yield: 64 biscuits

2¼ cups water
½ cup and 1 tsp. sugar
½ cup shortening
1 tbls. salt
2 packages yeast
2 eggs, beaten
8 cups flour
Butter
Sugar water

Boil 2 cups water, and mix it with ½ cup sugar, shortening, and salt./ Soften yeast in ¼ cup lukewarm water with 1 teaspoon sugar./ Stir yeast into first mixture./ Add beaten eggs, and stir in 4 cups flour./ Beat mixture until smooth, and stir in remaining flour./ Knead dough approximately 10 minutes./ Place dough in greased bowl, grease top of dough, cover, and place in refrigerator for several hours or overnight./

Take as much dough as desired, and form into rolls./ Place rolls in warm place until doubled in volume./ Brush tops of rolls with butter and sugar water./ In a 375° F. oven bake rolls for 15 to 20 minutes./ Remaining dough will keep in refrigerator for the next day./

Dilly Bread

Yield: 4 loaves

2 packages yeast
¼ cup warm water
2 cups creamed cottage
  cheese
Butter
2 eggs
4 tbls. sugar
2 tbls. minced dried onion
2 tsp. dill seed
2 tsp. dill weed
2 tsp. salt
½ tsp. baking soda
4½ to 5 cups flour
Onion salt

Dissolve yeast in warm water./ Heat cottage cheese and 2 tablespoons butter to lukewarm, and place in a large bowl with eggs, sugar, onion, dill seed, dill weed, salt, and baking soda./ Add yeast./ Slowly mix in enough flour to make a soft dough./ Knead dough, and let it rise 45 to 60 minutes in a warm place, covering bowl with cloth./ Punch dough down, and divide it into 4 parts./ Shape quarters into flattened balls, and put each in a well greased one quart casserole./ Cover each ball and let it rise in a warm place for 30 minutes./ In a 350° F. oven bake for 25 to 30 minutes, or until bread is browned./ Brush top of bread with butter and sprinkle with onion salt./

Crunchy "Granola"

4 cups old-fashioned rolled
oats
1 cup unsweetened shredded
coconut
¾ cup shelled sunflower
seeds
½ cup wheat germ
¼ cup sesame seeds
⅔ cup light honey
¼ cup vegetable oil
1 tbls. vanilla extract
1 cup blanched slivered
almonds (or cashews)
½ cup seedless raisins

Mix oats, coconut, sunflower seeds, wheat germ, and sesame seeds in a large mixing bowl./ In a small bowl, combine honey, oil, and vanilla and add to oat mixture a little at a time, stirring well after each addition./

In a lightly oiled or nonstick-finished large baking pan, spread cereal evenly./ In a 250° F. oven bake cereal for 1½ hours, stirring every 15 to 20 minutes, until cereal is light brown./ Toast nuts in a heavy, ungreased skillet./ Add nuts to cereal mixture and bake an additional 15 minutes./ Remove pan from oven, and cool completely./ Add raisins and store cereal in airtight container./

Whole Wheat Challah-Bread

1 quart water
1 oz. yeast
½ cup oil
4 oz. honey
3 eggs
1 tbls. lecithin
14 cups whole wheat flour
3 tbls. salt
Poppy seeds

Dissolve yeast in half the water, heated to approximately 115°F./ Let yeast sit for 5 minutes, and then add oil, honey, eggs (saving a little of the egg to brush on top), lecithin and the rest of the water./ Mix ingredients well./ Add salt and enough flour to make a dough of good consistency./ Knead dough well, and let it rise in a covered bowl 1½ to 2 hours./ Punch dough down, and knead it a second time./ Let dough rise again./

Divide dough and make into two loaves./ Place loaves in greased pans, and let them rise./ Brush tops with egg and sprinkle with poppy seeds./ In a hot oven, 375 to 400° F., bake bread approximately 35 to 40 minutes, or until done./

Passover Bagels

3 cups boiling water
1 cup chicken fat
½ tsp. sugar
½ tsp. salt
4 cups matzo meal
8 eggs

In a bowl, combine boiling water with chicken fat, sugar and salt, mixing until completely dissolved./ Add matzo meal and eggs and mix thoroughly./

Grease a baking pan with chicken fat./ Place 2 large tablespoons of batter on pan and shape hole in center./ Repeat process until all batter is used./ In a 400° F. oven, bake bagels until golden brown./

Iron Skillet Bread

4 cups flour
1 cup sugar
4 tsp. baking powder
1 tsp. salt
½ cup butter
1 cup light cream
1 cup golden raisins
½ cup milk
2 eggs
2 tbls. caraway seeds

In a bowl, mix together flour, sugar, baking powder and salt./ Cut in butter with pastry blender or two knives./ Add cream, raisins, milk, eggs and caraway seeds and mix well./ Spoon batter into well-greased iron skillet./ In a 350° F. oven, bake for one hour and 15 minutes./ Cool on rack before slicing./

Soft Roll Dough

Yield: 18 rolls

½ cake yeast
1 cup warm water or milk,
 approximately 80° F.
1 egg, beaten
¼ cup shortening
3 tbls. sugar
1½ tsp. salt
3½ to 4 cups flour
Egg wash

In a large bowl, dissolve yeast in warm water or milk./ Add egg, shortening, sugar and salt and stir until well blended./ Add 2 cups flour, one at a time, beating until smooth after each addition./ Add the third cup of flour and continue beating until dough is smooth and elastic./

Sprinkle half of remaining flour on board and turn dough out./ With floured hands, knead dough until it forms a smooth ball and is not sticky./ Place in lightly greased mixing bowl, grease top of dough lightly and cover with clean dish cloth./ In a preheated 200° F. oven that has been turned off, place pan of hot water on lower shelf and let dough rise on upper shelf for approximately 45 to 60 minutes, until doubled in size./ Punch dough down folding it over from bottom to top and side to side until most of the gas has been expelled./ Cover, and return to oven to rest for 15 minutes more./

Place dough on lightly floured surface and divide into 18 pieces./ Shape as desired or use any of the forms shown at left./ Place rolls in lightly greased pan, seam-side down./ Brush with egg wash./ Return once more to warm oven until almost double in size./ In a 400 to 425° F. oven, bake rolls for approximately 10 minutes or until golden brown./

Professor Sieverding
S.C.C.C. Department of Hotel Technology

Relishes and Preserves

Banana Jam

Yield: 7-8 oz. jars

3 cups ripe bananas
3 medium lemons
3 cups sugar
3 cups water
Dried ginger
Whole cloves

In a bowl, crush ripe bananas to a fine pulp./ Wash lemons, remove rind with a vegetable peeler, and slice rind into paper-thin strips./ Into a small dish, squeeze the juice from the lemons./ In a large kettle, combine sugar and water and boil for 10 minutes./ Add bananas, lemon juice and rind, a whole piece of dried ginger and a few cloves./ Cook mixture slowly for ½ to ¾ hour, stirring with a wooden spoon./ Remove ginger./ Mixture will be a pale-yellow mush./ Pour into sterilized jars and seal with paraffin./

Zucchini Pickle

Yield: 4 pints

2 lbs. fresh firm zucchini,
thinly sliced
2 small onions, quartered
and sliced
Water
½ cup non-iodized salt
3 cups cider vinegar
2 cups sugar
2 tsp. mustard seed
1 tsp. celery salt
1 tsp. tumeric

Place zucchini and onions in a bowl, and cover with water to one inch above the vegetables./ Add salt./ Let vegetables stand 2 hours, then drain thoroughly./

In a saucepan, combine vinegar, sugar, mustard seed, celery salt, and tumeric./ Bring ingredients to a boil, then pour over zucchini and onions./ Let mixture stand 2 hours./

Bring entire mixture to a boil, and cook for 5 minutes./ Place pickle in canning or regular jars./

Chutney

Yield: 2 to 3 quarts

4 lbs. apples, peeled and
chopped
1 large onion, chopped
1¼ lbs. brown sugar (or
1 cup white sugar plus ¼
cup molasses)
½ lb. seedless raisins
2 cups cider vinegar
⅔ cup crystallized ginger,
chopped (or ginger root,
chopped)
2 tbls. chili powder
2 tbls. mustard seed
1 tbls. salt
1 tsp. tarragon vinegar
1 small clove garlic (or
½ tsp. garlic powder)

In a large saucepan, combine apples, onion, brown sugar, raisins, cider vinegar, ginger, chili powder, mustard seed, salt, tarragon vinegar and garlic and bring mixture to a boil./ Lower heat and simmer chutney for one hour./ Place chutney in hot sterilized jars, and seal./

Peach Jam

Yield: 12 to 14—6 oz. jars

12 peaches, peeled, halved
  and pitted
4 navel oranges, quartered
1 lemon, quartered and
  seeded
Sugar

Chop fruit, or put through medium blade of food chopper./ Measure volume of fruit, and add an equal measure of sugar to it./ Stir fruit and sugar together, and let mixture stand overnight./

In a large 8 to 10 quart pot, bring fruit mixture to a boil./ Boil 20 minutes, stirring with a long-handled wooden spoon./ Skim jam with metal spoon./ Pour into sterilized jars, and seal with paraffin./

Old Fashioned Dill Pickles

Yield: 4 quarts

⅔ gallon water
2½ tbls. salt
8 to 10 cloves garlic,
  unpeeled and crushed
  slightly with the side of a
  heavy knife
3 sprigs fresh dill
Pickling cucumbers
1 slice rye bread

In a one gallon jar, dissolve salt in water./ Add garlic and dill./ Pack the jar firmly with cucumbers./ Add enough water to cover all the cucumbers./ Place rye bread on top of cucumbers, and then place a clean board or small plate, and well scrubbed flat rock on top of the bread to keep pickles submerged./

Keep pickles at room temperature 3 to 6 days, until they have stopped bubbling./ After 3 days, taste the brine and, if necessary, add salt to taste./ When pickles are done, remove garlic cloves from jar and refrigerate pickles./

Edgewood Inn

Green Cucumber Relish

Yield: 8 quarts

½ peck medium cucumbers,
  peeled and finely chopped
2 onions, finely chopped
⅓ cup salt
2 cups vinegar
½ cup brown sugar
1 rounded tbls. celery seed
1 rounded tbls. mustard seed
1 rounded tbls. ground
  mustard
⅛ tsp. cayenne pepper

In two separate bowls, salt cucumbers and onions and let them stand overnight./ Drain, and mix vetetables together./ (If vegetables are too salty, rinse them under cold running water and drain again.)/ In a kettle, combine cucumbers and onions with vinegar, brown sugar, celery seed, mustard seed, ground mustard and cayenne, and boil for 10 minutes./ Can relish./

Sweet Chunk Pickles

Yield: 4 quarts

7 lbs. fresh cucumber, 6 to 8
  inches long and not too
  thick
Brine (approximately 6 tbls.
  salt to each quart water)
Water
Vinegar
Walnut-sized piece of alum
3 lbs. sugar
1 oz. allspice
1 oz. cinnamon
1 oz. celery seeds

Wash cucumbers and pack them in crock./ Cover cucumbers with brine strong enough to float an egg./ Let cucumbers stand 3 days./ Pour off brine and cover cucumbers with fresh water./ Let them stand 3 more days, changing water if it becomes slimy./ Wipe cucumbers dry, and cut them into round chunks one inch thick./

Scald cucumber chunks in weak vinegar with a piece of alum./ Drain cucumber and return chunks to crock, discarding vinegar./ Mix sugar, allspice, cinnamon and celery seeds with sufficient vinegar to more than cover cucumber./ Boil vinegar mixture 3 minutes, then pour it over cucumber./ The following day, pour vinegar syrup into saucepan and boil again, until thickened./ Pour syrup over cucumber./

The crock need not be sealed; chunk pickles can be stored and used from crock./ They will keep at least a year./

Miss Decker's Tomato Catsup

Yield: 4 quarts

1 gallon tomatoes, strained
1 quart onions, sliced
½ cup sugar
1½ tbls. black peppercorns
1 tbls. whole cloves
1 tbls. celery seed
1-2 inch stick cinnamon
2 cups cider vinegar
4 tbls. coarse salt

In a large pot, combine tomatoes and onions and boil until soft./ Strain mixture, and add sugar to it./ Place peppercorns, cloves, celery seed and cinnamon stick in a cheesecloth bag, tie it closed, and place in the tomato-onion mixture./ Boil mixture quickly, stirring with a wooden spoon, until reduced by half./ Remove spice bag from pot, and add vinegar and salt to the catsup./ Boil 10 additional minutes./ Bottle catsup immediately, sealing with wax./

Blueberry Jam

Yield: 4 pints

2 quarts blueberries,
  destemmed
6 cups sugar

Wash and drain blueberries./ Place berries in a large, 8 to 10 quart pot and cook over low heat until boiling, then simmer one minute./ With a wooden spoon, add sugar to the berries, stirring until sugar dissolves./ Boil jam rapidly until thickened, stirring occasionally./ Skim jam's surface with metal spoon./ Pour blueberry jam into hot, sterilized jars, and seal jars with paraffin./

Kay's Sliced Green Tomatoes Pickle

Yield: 4 to 6 quarts

1 peck green tomatoes
6 onions
Salt
1 quart vinegar
2 lbs. brown sugar
2 heaping tbls. mixed
  whole pickling spices

Slice tomatoes and onions, and place in large bowl./ Sprinkle them with salt and let stand overnight./ Drain vegetables./ Scald them with water, to which a little vinegar has been added./ Drain again./

In a large pot, combine vinegar, brown sugar, and spices, and bring to a boil./ When mixture reaches boiling point, add tomatoes and onions and cook until vegetables are tender./ Seal pickle in hot clean jars./

Corn Relish

Yield: 5 pints

9 cups fresh corn kernels
3 cups cider vinegar
2 cups onion, chopped
1 cup sweet green peppers,
  chopped
1 cup sugar
½ cup sweet red peppers,
  chopped
2 tbls. salt
1½ tbls. celery seed
1½ tbls. dry mustard

In a Dutch oven or large saucepan, combine all ingredients and bring to a boil./ Simmer 15 minutes, stirring occasionally./ Pour into hot, sterilized jars./

Relish

Yield: 3 to 4 quarts

2 quarts cabbage, chopped
  and shredded
2 quarts green tomatoes, cut
  into eighths
4 large onions, chopped
3 red peppers, combination
  of sweet and hot, chopped
3½ cups sugar
2 cups vinegar
2 oz. mustard seed
3 tbls. salt
1 tsp. tumeric
1 tsp. ground cloves
1 tsp. cinnamon

In a large saucepan, combine cabbage, tomatoes, onions, peppers, sugar, vinegar, mustard seed, salt, tumeric, cloves, and cinnamon./ Bring ingredients to a boil, then cook relish half an hour./ Place relish in hot, sterilized jars, and seal./

Kay's Chili Sauce

Yield: 2 quarts

24 ripe tomatoes
4 green peppers
4 large onions
4 cups vinegar
4 cups sugar
1 tbls. salt
1 tsp. ginger powder
1 tsp. cinnamon
½ tsp. cloves

Chop tomatoes, green peppers, and onions in a food chopper./ In a large covered saucepan, boil chopped vegetables with vinegar, sugar, salt, ginger, cinnamon, and cloves for 2 to 3 hours, or until sauce is thick./ Stir constantly to prevent sauce from sticking to pan./

Sauerkraut

Yield: 4 quarts

12 lbs. heavy, white, packed
  heads of cabbage
7 tbls. coarse salt

Shred cabbage finely, reserving 2 or 3 leaves, and discarding cores./ In a 10 quart pot, mix half the cabbage with half the salt, combining thoroughly./ Using a short length of wood, pound the cabbage until brine runs freely./ Place cabbage and brine in an earthenware crock large enough to allow for overflow and repeat process with remaining ingredients./ Press cabbage down firmly after each layer./

Cover with reserved cabbage leaves./ Place a board or heavy plate over leaves and weigh it down with a rock./ Set crock in a dark spot at room temperature and allow to ferment for 8 days./ Skim mold from surface and remove leaves before serving./

Spiced Watermelon Rind

Yield: 3 pints

3 lbs. white portion of
  watermelon, cubed
Salted water
5 cups sugar
2 cups cider vinegar
1 cup cold water
1 lemon, sliced
1 tbls. whole cloves
1 tbls. whole allspice
1 tbls. cinnamon stick,
  broken

In a large kettle, let watermelon stand in salted water to cover overnight, (2 tablespoons salt to one quart fresh water)./ Drain, cover watermelon with fresh cold water, and cook until tender./ Drain again./

In a large saucepan, combine sugar, vinegar and cold water./ Tie cloves, allspice, cinnamon and lemon slices in a cheesecloth bag and add to saucepan./ Bring mixture to boil and boil 5 minutes./ Add watermelon and cook until transparent, approximately 45 minutes./ Pack in hot, sterilized jars./

Sweet Cucumber Pickles

Yield: 2 to 3 quarts

2 quarts cucumbers, peeled
  and thinly sliced
1 large onion, thinly sliced
  (additional onion optional)
Brine
3 cups vinegar
2 cups sugar, white or brown
1 cup water
2 tbls. white mustard seed
1 tbls. whole allspice

Cover cucumbers and onion (add additional onion if stronger onion flavor is desired) with brine and let mixture stand overnight./ Drain./ In a large pot, combine vinegar, sugar, water, mustard seed and allspice and bring to a boil./ Add cucumbers and onion and cook until vegetables are transparent, or easily pierced with a fork./ Pack in hot sterile jars and seal at once./

Apple Butter

Yield: 3 to 4 quarts

6 lbs. apples
2 quarts apple juice or
  cider
3 cups sugar
1½ tsp. cinnamon
½ tsp. ground cloves
½ tsp. nutmeg
½ tsp. allspice

Wash apples, remove stems, and quarter./ In a large kettle, combine apples with apple juice or cider and cook slowly until soft./ Put apples through a fine strainer or food mill./ Measure 3 quarts of pulp, return pulp to kettle and stir in sugar and spices./ Cook mixture over low heat, stirring constantly, until sugar is dissolved./ Turn up heat and cook rapidly until apple butter sheets from a spoon./ Pour into sterilized jars and seal./

Mustard Pickles

Yield: 7 pints

3 quarts hot water
1 quart cabbage, shredded
1 quart onions, chopped
1 quart green tomatoes,
  diced
1 quart unpeeled cucumbers,
  sliced
4 large green peppers,
  chopped
6 hot green peppers,
  chopped
2 sweet red peppers,
  chopped
1 cup salt
1 quart cider vinegar
1 cup sugar
½ cup prepared mustard
½ cup flour
2 tsp. celery seed

In a large kettle, combine hot water, cabbage, onions, green tomatoes, cucumbers, green peppers, hot green peppers, red peppers and salt and let stand for 8 hours, stirring occasionally./ Drain off liquid, rinse under cold water and drain vegetables again./ In a separate pan, combine vinegar, sugar, mustard, flour and celery seed and blend well./ Cook mixture until thick, add vegetables and bring to a boil./ Remove from heat and pack at once in sterilized jars and seal./

Desserts

Orange-Coconut Mold
Serves 8

½ cup water
½ cup orange juice
1-3 oz. package orange-
flavored gelatin
½ cup rose' wine (or any fruit
juice)
½ cup heavy cream,
whipped
1 banana, sliced
1 orange, sectioned
½ cup shredded coconut
Leaf lettuce
Oranges, sliced (optional)

In a saucepan, combine water and orange juice and bring to a boil./ Pour boiling liquid over gelatin and stir until gelatin dissolves./ Let cool./ Add wine or fruit juice to mixture, and refrigerate until it forms mounds when dropped from spoon./ Beat with a rotary beater until mixture is fluffy./ Fold in whipped cream./ Add banana, orange sections, and shredded coconut, and blend into mixture./ Pour into greased one quart mold, and refrigerate until firm./ Line platter with lettuce and unmold dessert; decorate with sliced oranges if desired./

Mint Sherbet
Serves 8

3 pints lemon sherbet
⅓ cup creme de menthe (or
¾ tsp. mint flavoring and 3
to 4 drops green food
coloring)

In the large bowl of an electric mixer, soften sherbet and then beat it quickly./ Blend in creme de menthe./ Fill sherbet cups with sherbet, and freeze dessert./ Serve when desired./

Baked Apples With Apricot Meringue
Serves 6

6 golden delicious apples,
peeled and cored
6 tbls. raisins and chopped
nuts
⅔ cup sugar
6 tsp. butter (or margarine)
⅓ cup sweet vermouth
Water
2 tsp. lemon juice
1 cup plus 2 tbls. apricot jam
(or apricot preserves),
strained
2 egg whites
¼ tsp. vanilla extract

Place apples in baking pan and fill with raisins and nuts./ Sprinkle ⅓ cup sugar over apples, then top each with one teaspoon butter./ Mix vermouth and sufficient water to make ½ cup liquid, and pour over apples, then sprinkle lemon juice over them./ In a 350° F. oven, bake apples, basting with vermouth and water from pan, for 30 to 40 minutes./ When apples are tender, place them on an oven-proof platter./ Reserve juice in baking pan./

Beat egg whites, gradually adding ⅓ cup sugar, until stiff peaks form./ Add vanilla to meringue./ Cover apples with one cup strained apricot jam, then coat each with meringue./ In a 450°F. oven bake apples for 2 minutes, or until meringue is lightly browned./

In a saucepan over low heat, stir juices from oven pan with 2 tablespoons apricot jam./ Spoon sauce over apples and serve./

Ribbon Salad

Serves 24

2-3 oz. packages lime gelatin
5 cups hot water
4 cups cold water
1-3 oz. package lemon
  gelatin
½ cup miniature
  marshmallows
1 cup pineapple juice
8 oz. cream cheese (room
  temperature)
1-1 lb. 4 oz. can crushed
  pineapple
1 cup heavy cream, whipped
1 cup mayonnaise
2-3 oz. packages cherry
  gelatin

Dissolve lime gelatin in 2 cups hot water./ Add 2 cups cold water, and pour mixture into 14 by 10 by 2 inch pan./ Chill until partially set./

In the top of a double boiler, dissolve lemon gelatin in one cup hot water./ Add marshmallows and stir to melt./ Remove mixture from heat, and add pineapple juice and cream cheese./ Beat until well blended./ Add crushed pineapple, and cool mixture slightly./ Fold in whipped cream and mayonnaise, and chill until thick./ Pour lemon gelatin mixture over lime gelatin, and chill until almost set./

Dissolve cherry gelatin in 2 cups hot water./ Add 2 cups cold water and chill gelatin until it is syrupy./ Pour cherry gelatin over lemon gelatin layer./ Chill ribbon salad until firm./ Unmold to serve./ Recipe makes 24 servings./ (Ribbon salad may be made with other gelatin flavors if desired.)/

Mousse-In-A-Minute

Serves 5 to 6

¾ cup plus 1 tbls. milk
½ tsp. instant coffee powder
1-6 oz. package chocolate
  chips
2 eggs
3 tbls. rum (or Tia Maria)

Scald milk with instant coffee./ Place chocolate chips in blender, and add scalded milk mixture, blending until smooth./ Without turning off blender, add eggs and rum, and blend ingredients for 2 minutes./ Pour mixture into individual demi-tasse cups or a glass dish; cover containers./ Chill mousse for several hours or overnight./

Candy Apples

Yield: 12 to 14 apples

12 to 14 hard, small apples
  (Jonathans, Cortlands, N.
  Spy, Stamens, Delicious,
  Baldwins, etc.)
Skewers or popsickle sticks
1 cup light corn syrup
1 cup sugar
½ to ¾ cup water
4 capfuls red food coloring
1 tbls. food flavoring (cherry,
  raspberry, or strawberry)

De-stem apples, and polish them with towel./ Place skewer sticks into underside of apples./ Grease cookie sheet large enough to accommodate all dipped apples./

In a deep, narrow pot, thoroughly mix corn syrup, sugar, water, and food coloring./ Using confectionary thermometer, heat mixture to crack, at 290° F./ Lower heat to 285° F. and add food flavoring./ Quickly dip apples in mixture, wiping the dripping from each apple by twisting it and rubbing it against pot rim./ Place dipped apples on cookie sheet and allow coating to harden./

Raspberry Mold

Serves 8

2-10 oz. packages frozen
  raspberries, defrosted
Water
2-3 oz. packages raspberry-
  flavored gelatin
1 cup sour cream
2 ripe bananas, sliced

Drain liquid from raspberries./ Add enough water to the raspberry juice to equal 3½ cups./ Boil 2 cups of this liquid and add to raspberry gelatin, stirring to dissolve gelatin./ Add remaining 1½ cups of juice and water to gelatin, and refrigerate mixture until partially set./ Fold raspberries into gelatin, and pour half this mixture into a greased 1½ quart mold./ Refrigerate until firm./ Do not refrigerate remaining raspberry and gelatin mixture, but keep it in a cool place./

Remove mold from refrigerator, and spoon on a layer of sour cream./ Top sour cream with a layer of sliced bananas./ Add remaining gelatin and raspberries to top of mold, and replace in refrigerator until firm./ Serve when desired, on platter garnished with watercress and fruit of your choice./

Blueberry Grunt

Serves 4

2 cups blueberries
½ cup water
⅛ tsp. allspice
Sugar (or artificial sweetener)
Baking powder biscuit dough
  (or unbaked biscuits)
Heavy cream

Cook together blueberries, water and allspice until mixture is soft./ Sweeten with sugar to taste./ Pour mixture into a deep baking dish with cover./ Place biscuit dough on top./ Cover baking dish./

Set dish in a deep pot of boiling water./ Cover pot and cook for one hour on top of stove, keeping the water at a constant boil./ Add more water as necessary to keep water level within one inch of the top of the baking dish./

Serve blueberry grunt from the dish with heavy cream spooned over./

Wine And Black Cherry Mold

Serves 6 to 8

3 cups boiling water
2-6 oz. packages black cherry
  gelatin
2-16 oz. cans pitted black
  cherries
Water
1 cup sweet grape wine
½ cup chopped walnuts

Pour boiling water into a large bowl, add gelatin, and stir until gelatin dissolves./ Drain cherries, reserving juice./ Add enough water to juice to make 2 cups liquid./ Add juice and wine to gelatin mixture, and place in refrigerator./ When partially set, add cherries and chopped walnuts./ Pour mixture into large mold, and chill./ (This mold is best made 2 or 3 days in advance, so wine can be absorbed by the cherries.)/

Snow Pudding

Serves 6 to 8

2 tbls. (or 2 envelopes)
  unflavored gelatin
2½ cups water
1¾ cups sugar
½ cup lemon juice
3 eggs, separated
2 cups milk
1 tsp. vanilla extract
1/8 tsp. salt

Custard Sauce
3 egg yolks
¼ cup sugar
2 cups milk
1 tsp. vanilla extract
⅛ tsp. salt

In a bowl, soften gelatin in ½ cup cold water./ Pour in 2 cups boiling water, and stir until gelatin is dissolved./ Add 1½ cups sugar to the mixture, and stir until sugar dissolves./ Stir in the lemon juice./ Chill mixture until partially set, then beat until frothy./

Beat egg whites until stiff, and fold them into gelatin./ Pour mixture into a lightly oiled one quart mold or bowl./ Chill until firm./

Beat egg yolks and combine with sugar and salt in the top of a double boiler./ Scald milk, and add it slowly to egg yolk mixture, stirring constantly, until mixture coats spoon./ Do not allow it to boil./ Pour custard sauce into a small bowl./ Cover bowl and cool sauce./ Serve custard sauce spooned over chilled snow pudding./

Kentucky Bourbon Balls

Yield: 6 dozen

3¼ cups confectioner's sugar
½ cup butter or margarine,
  softened
8 tsp. bourbon
¾ cup pecans or black
  walnuts, chopped
1½ lbs. semi-sweet
  chocolate, grated

In a bowl, cream sugar, butter and bourbon until smooth./ Add nuts and mix well./ Form mixture into ¾ inch balls./ (If mixture is too soft, add more sugar slowly.)/ Place balls on metal tray and refrigerate one to 1½ hours./

In the top of a double boiler over hot water, melt chocolate./ Remove top of double boiler, fill bottom with warm water (approximately 85°F.), and replace top./ Spear each bourbon ball with a fork and dip into chocolate, allowing excess to drip off./ Drop balls onto wax paper and spread on racks./ When firm, pack into airtight containers./

Orange Yogurt Ice Cream

Yield: ½ gallon

4 cups orange yogurt
2 cups frozen concentrated
  orange juice
1½ cups sugar
⅛ tsp. salt
4 egg whites, beaten

Combine yogurt, orange juice, sugar, and salt in an electric blender./ Mix ingredients until well blended./ Freeze mixture to a "mushy" consistency./ Add beaten egg whites, and mix well./ Freeze ice cream until firm./

Fudge

Yield: 2 pounds

4 cups sugar
1 ⅓ cups milk
4 squares unsweetened
chocolate
¼ cup light corn syrup
5 tbls. butter or margarine
1 cup pecans, broken
1 tbls. vanilla

In a saucepan over low heat, combine sugar, milk, chocolate and corn syrup./ Stir while increasing heat to medium until well blended./ Increase heat and cook without stirring until candy thermometer reads 236°F. or until mixture forms a soft ball in cold water./ Remove pan from heat and add butter without stirring./ Let cool to lukewarm (110°F.), then beat with electric mixer until smooth./ Continue beating with wooden spoon until mixture becomes dull-looking./ Add pecans and vanilla./ Pour into wax paper-lined pan./ With a spoon, make swirls on top of fudge./ Let stand until firm./

Maple Frango

Serves 8

3 egg yolks
½ cup maple syrup, boiling
2 cups heavy cream,
whipped

Beat egg yolks until they are thick and lemon colored./ Slowly pour boiling maple syrup into yolks, beating constantly./ Transfer mixture to a saucepan and cook it, stirring, until thickened./ Do not let mixture boil./ Let cool and fold in whipped cream./ Freeze dessert 3 or 4 hours./

Coffee Mousse

Serves 10 to 12

32 marshmallows
1½ cups strong coffee
3 cups heavy cream
1 square bitter chocolate,
shaved

In the top of a double boiler, melt marshmallows in coffee./ Cool mixture./ Whip cream./ With a rubber spatula, fold coffee mixture into whipped cream (do not add cream to coffee mixture!)./ Place mousse in a deep serving dish, and sprinkle top with shaved chocolate./ Chill until serving./

Bananas Foster

Serves 6

½ cup butter
6 tbls. light brown sugar
3 ripe, firm bananas
⅔ cup Puerto Rican rum,
warmed
2 tbls. cognac
Vanilla ice cream

Melt butter in a skillet, and stir in brown sugar./ Cook over low heat for 5 minutes./ Cut the bananas in half lengthwise, then crosswise./ Add banana quarters to pan, and cook until browned on all sides./ Remove skillet from heat, add warmed rum and cognac and set aflame./ Pour bananas over ice cream./

Old-Fashioned Creamy Rice Pudding

Serves 6

1 quart milk
¼ tsp. salt
½ cup long grain rice
½ cup raisins
2 eggs
1 cup evaporated milk
½ cup sugar
1 tsp. vanilla
Nutmeg (or cinnamon sugar)
  (optional)

In a heavy saucepan, heat milk and salt to simmer./ Stir in rice, and simmer for 15 minutes, stirring occasionally./ Add raisins to pan, and cook approximately 5 minutes longer, or until rice is tender./

In a bowl, beat eggs with evaporated milk, sugar, and vanilla./ Blend several spoonfuls of cooked rice, one at a time, into bowl, then return contents of bowl to saucepan and cook mixture slowly until it thickens slightly./

Pour pudding into bowl, stirring often while it cools./ Serve warm or cold with a sprinkling of nutmeg or cinnamon sugar, if desired./

Windsor Hotel

Zabaglione (Marsala Custard)

Serves 6

8 egg yolks
½ cup fine sugar
1 cup Marsala (or sherry)
  wine

In the top of a double boiler, beat egg yolks and sugar with a wire whisk until thick./ Beat in the wine./ Set pot over hot water, and beat mixture until it is hot and very thick./ Do not let mixture boil./ Spoon zabaglione into tall glasses or sherbet cups, and serve./

The Grotto Restaurant

Candied Grapefruit Peel

Yield: Approximately ½ pound

Peel of 3 to 4 grapefruits
2 quarts water
2 tsp. salt
2½ cups sugar
Food coloring (optional)

Wash grapefruit peel, drain and cut into strips 3 by ½ inch./ In a bowl, combine 7 cups of water with salt and pour over peel./ Let stand 8 to 10 hours./ Pour mixture into a large saucepan and boil for 10 minutes, then drain peel./ In another saucepan, combine sugar with one cup water and boil until syrup spins a thread (232 to 234°F.)./ If desired, tint with 7 drops yellow and one drop green food coloring./ Add grapefruit peel to syrup and cook slowly for 30 minutes./ Remove peel from syrup and lay on wax paper to dry for one hour. Roll in sugar if desired./

Methodist Goodies Candy

Yield: approximately 50 candies

1-6 oz. package butterscotch
  bits (or chocolate bits)
½ cup peanut butter
1 medium can chow mein
  noodles
1 cup miniature
  marshmallows

Melt butterscotch bits and peanut butter over hot water./ Add chow mein noodles and marshmallows and mix./ Cool mixture slightly, and drop candy by teaspoonfuls onto waxed paper, or press candy into buttered pan./

Lemon Ice Cream

Yield: ½ gallon

2 cups sugar
¼ cup fresh lemon juice
1 tbls. lemon rind, grated
5 cups heavy cream
¼ tsp. yellow food coloring

Combine sugar, lemon juice, and lemon rind./ Whip cream lightly, and add it to lemon mixture./ Add food coloring and mix well./ Pour mixture into lemon shells or mold, and freeze ice cream./

Fresh Blueberry Pudding

Serves 6

2 cups blueberries, picked
  over, rinsed and drained
Juice of one lemon
½ tsp. cinnamon
1¼ cup sugar
3 tbls. butter
½ cup milk
1 cup flour
1 tsp. baking powder
¼ tsp. salt
1 tbls. cornstarch
Salt
1 cup boiling water

In a bowl, mix together blueberries, lemon juice and cinnamon and place in a well-buttered 8 inch square pan./ In another bowl cream butter and ¾ cup sugar./ Add milk./ Sift together flour, baking powder and salt and add to mixture./ Spread batter over blueberries./ Mix together remaining ½ cup sugar, cornstarch and a dash of salt and sprinkle over batter./ Pour boiling water over top, but do not stir./ In a 375°F. oven, bake for one hour./ Serve warm with whipped cream./

Passover Fruit Candy

Yield: 2 pounds

½ lb. pitted prunes
½ lb. dried apricots
¼ lb. golden raisins
¼ lb. candied orange peel
¼ lb. candied grapefruit peel
¼ lb. Passover bittersweet
  chocolate, melted
1 tbls. brandy
Sugar

Grind together the prunes, apricots, raisins, orange peel and grapefruit peel./ Add chocolate and brandy and mix together well with hands./ Roll mixture into logs, cut into one inch slices and roll into balls. Roll in sugar and store in a dry place./ This candy lasts indefinitely and improves with age./

Pies, Cakes and Cookies

Shelley Ooogan

Peanut Butter Pie

1 cup light or dark corn syrup
1 cup sugar
3 eggs, lightly beaten
⅓ cup chunk-style peanut
  butter
½ tsp vanilla
1-9 inch unbaked pastry
  shell
1 cup heavy cream, whipped

Combine corn syrup, sugar, eggs, peanut butter and vanilla and mix until thoroughly blended./ Pour into pastry shell./ In a 400°F. oven, bake for 15 minutes./ Reduce heat to 350°F. and bake 30 to 35 minutes longer./ (Filling will appear slightly looser in center.)/ Cool pie, then chill./ Serve topped with whipped cream./

Brandy Alexander Pie

1 envelope unflavored
  gelatin
½ cup cold water
⅔ cup sugar
3 eggs, separated
⅛ tsp. salt
¼ cup cognac
¼ cup creme de Cocoa
2 cups heavy cream,
  whipped
1-9 inch graham cracker
  crust
Bittersweet chocolate curls
  (optional)

In a saucepan, sprinkle gelatin over cold water./ Add ⅓ cup sugar, egg yolks and salt, stirring to blend./ Heat mixture over low heat, stirring, until gelatin dissolves and mixture thickens slightly./ Do not boil!/ Remove from heat and stir in cognac and creme de Cocoa./ Refrigerate until mixture mounds slightly like pudding./

Beat egg whites until stiff with remaining ⅓ cup sugar./ Fold into chilled mixture./ Fold in one cup whipped cream./ Turn into pie crust and chill overnight./ Garnish with remaining one cup whipped cream and chocolate curls, if desired, before serving./

Lemon Chiffon Pie

1-14 oz. can sweetened
  condensed milk
½ cup lemon juice
5 egg whites
2 tbls. sugar
1 tbls. lemon rind, grated
1-9 inch pie shell
  (graham cracker or
  baked pastry)

In a bowl, combine milk and lemon juice, stirring until thick and smooth./ Beat egg whites until foamy, then add sugar, a tablespoon at a time, and continue beating until stiff peaks form./ Fold into milk-lemon juice mixture./ Sprinkle lemon rind on bottom of pie shell./ Pour filling into shell and chill until set./ (Pie may also be frozen.)/

Easy Apple Crumb Pie

1½ cups flour
¾ cup sugar
1½ tsp. baking powder
¼ tsp. salt
4 tbls. butter or other
  shortening
1 egg
2 cups apple sauce

Into a mixing bowl, sift together flour, sugar, baking powder and salt./ Cut in butter or shortening with two knives./ Add egg and mix until dough is crumbly./ Press half of crumbs on bottom of a 9 inch pie pan./ Add apple sauce and cover with remaining crumbs./ In a 350° F. oven, bake pie for one hour./

Old Fashioned Apple Pie

3 cups flour
¾ cup sugar
2 tsp. baking powder
⅓ cup oil
2 eggs, beaten
2 to 3 tbls. orange juice or
  milk
2 tsp. vanilla
6 to 8 good-sized apples
  (Cortland)
Sugar
Cinnamon
Rind of one lemon, grated
Butter (optional)
Raisins (optional)

Into a mixing bowl, sift together flour, sugar and baking powder./ Add oil and stir until little crumbles have formed./ Add extra oil, if necessary, if all flour isn't absorbed./ Add eggs, juice or milk and vanilla and mix well until dough forms a ball dry enough to handle./ (If dough seems too dry, add small amounts of additional liquid until it reaches proper consistency; if too wet, add small amounts of flour.)/ Knead a few times until nice and spongy./ Cut dough in half./ Roll each half out on a floured surface into a rectangle 12 by 8 inches./

Slice apples./ Sprinkle with sugar and cinnamon to taste./ Place one dough rectangle in bottom of a 2 by 12 by 8 inch pan and top with apples./ Sprinkle with lemon rind./ If desired, dot with butter and mix in raisins./ Cover with top crust./ Poke crust with fork for steam vents./ In a 350° F. oven, bake pie for approximately one hour, or until crust is golden./

Date Nut Bread

1½ cups flour
1 cup raisins
1 cup dates, cut into small
  pieces
1 cup nuts, coarsely chopped
1 cup sugar
1 tsp. baking soda mixed with
  1 cup boiling water
1 egg

Mix all ingredients until well blended./ Pour into loaf pan which has been lined with wax paper./ In a 350° F. oven, bake for 50 to 60 minutes./ To serve, slice bread and spread with cream cheese./

Blueberry Tea Cake

2¼ cups flour
2 tsp. baking powder
½ tsp. salt
½ cup butter (or margarine)
1¼ cups sugar
1 egg
½ cup milk
2 cups blueberries
¼ tsp. cinnamon

Sift together 2 cups flour, baking powder, and salt./ Cream ¼ cup butter into sifted mixture./ Gradually add ¾ cup sugar./ Add egg and milk to batter, and beat until smooth./ Fold in blueberries./ Pour batter into greased and floured 8 by 9 inch pan./

Make crumb topping by combining ¼ cup melted butter with ½ cup sugar, ¼ cup flour, and cinnamon./ Sprinkle crumb topping over batter./ In a 350° F. oven, bake cake for 40 to 45 minutes./

Chocolate Chip Sour Cream Cake

Yield: 6-10" Cakes

1 cup vegetable shortening
1 cup butter
2 cups sugar
10 large eggs
2 cups sour cream
6 cups sifted cake flour
1½ tbls. baking powder
¾ tbls. baking soda
1 scant cup brown sugar
½ cup chopped nuts
¼ lb. chocolate chips
1½ tbls. cocoa
½ tbls. cinnamon

In a mixing bowl, cream shortening and butter with sugar./ With electric mixer on medium speed, add eggs slowly, beating well./ Blend in sour cream./ Add sifted flour, baking powder, and baking soda to batter, and mix well./

In a separate bowl, prepare filling by combining brown sugar, nuts, chocolate chips, cocoa, and cinnamon./ Pour half the batter into 6 greased 10 inch loaf pans./ Sprinkle half the filling over batter./ Pour remaining batter into pans, and sprinkle remaining filling on top./ In a 375° F. oven, bake loaves for 35 to 40 minutes./ Loaves freeze very well./ (Recipe may be cut in half for smaller yield.)/

Chef: Sam Ziewig   *Pines Hotel*

Pineapple Carrot Cake

3 cups sifted flour
2 tsp. baking soda
2 tsp. cinnamon
½ tsp. salt
2 cups sugar
1¼ cups cooking oil
2 tsp. vanilla
2 cups raw carrots, finely grated
1½ cups chopped nuts
1 cup crushed pineapple, well drained
3 eggs

Sift together flour, baking soda, cinnamon, and salt./ In large bowl, combine sugar, oil, and vanilla./ Blend in dry ingredients./ Add carrots, nuts, and pineapple, and mix well./ Add eggs one at a time, mixing well after each addition./

Pour batter into a well greased and floured tube pan./ In a 350° F. oven, bake cake for 70 minutes, or until cake springs back when pressed gently on top./ Cool cake upright in pan—do not invert!/ Cake tastes best when prepared several days in advance of serving./

Refrigerator Yeast Coffee Cake

Sugar
Salt
1-2 oz. cake yeast
3 eggs, separated
1 tsp. vanilla extract
1 cup salt butter, melted and
  cooled
¾ cup milk
3 cups flour
Cinnamon
½ cup chopped walnuts
1½ cups golden raisins,
  plumped

Streusel
3 tbls. butter
3 tbls. flour
2 tbls. sugar
1 tbls. bread crumbs
Cinnamon

In a warm bowl, place ½ cup sugar and a pinch of salt./ Crumble yeast into sugar./ Cover bowl and set aside in a warm place until yeast melts./ Watch yeast to be sure it is completely dissolved./ If necessary, stir mixture with spatula./ Add egg yolks and vanilla./ Combine cooled butter with milk and mix well./ Pour into mixture, stirring with spatula or wooden spoon./ Add flour and beat until dough is smooth./ Cover dough with waxed paper and towel./ Set bowl in warm place until dough is partially risen, volume being increased by approximately one third./ Cover bowl with towel and refrigerate overnight./

The following day, prepare streusel as directed below./ Then beat egg whites with ½ cup sugar until they are stiff but not dry./ Roll dough out flat./ Using a pastry brush, cover dough with half the egg white mixture./ Sprinkle dough with sugar, cinnamon, ground nuts, and raisins, in that order./ Roll dough up like a jelly roll./ Place roll in a greased and floured tube pan, with outside flap on inside of pan./ Overlap ends of roll in the pan./ Cover pan with towel and leave in a warm place (80°F.) about one hour, or until dough volume doubles./ Use remaining egg white mixture to cover top of dough./ Sprinkle streusel over top./ In a 375°F. oven bake cake for one hour./

Melt butter and with a fork mix in flour, sugar, bread crumbs, and cinnamon./ Refrigerate streusel before using./

Grandma's Mayonnaise Cake

2 cups cake flour
1 cup sugar
4 tbls. cocoa
2 scant tsp. baking soda
1 tsp. salt
1 cup mayonnaise
1 cup lukewarm water
1 tsp. vanilla extract

Into a bowl, sift together flour, sugar, cocoa, baking soda, and salt./ Add mayonnaise, water, and vanilla, and mix batter until well blended./ Pour batter into an 8 by 8 inch square, greased pan, and bake cake in a 350° F. oven for approximately 35 minutes./

Frost cake with mocha icing, made by adding one teaspoon of instant coffee to a confectioners' sugar-butter icing./

Maraschino Party Cake

2¼ cups cake flour
1 cup sugar
3 tsp. baking powder
1 tsp. salt
16 maraschino cherries, cut
  in eighths
½ cup shortening
½ cup milk
¼ cup cherry juice
4 egg whites, stiffly beaten
½ cup chopped nuts

In a bowl, sift together flour, sugar, baking powder, and salt./ Add cherry pieces, shortening, milk, and cherry juice to dry ingredients, and beat with mixer until smooth./ Fold in egg whites and nuts./ Pour batter into two greased and floured cake pans, and bake in a 350° F. oven for 30 to 35 minutes, or until cake tests done./ Cool in pans 10 to 15 minutes, then remove to wire rack./ Frost cooled cake if desired./

Carrot Cake

2 cups flour
1½ cups brown sugar
2 tsp. baking soda
2 tsp. cinnamon
½ tsp. salt
1¼ cups vegetable oil
3 eggs
2 tsp. vanilla
2 cups raw carrots, grated
1 cup raisins
1 cup walnuts

In a bowl, blend together flour, brown sugar, baking soda, cinnamon and salt./ Add oil, eggs and vanilla and mix into flour mixture./ Add carrots, raisins and walnuts and mix well./ Pour into 2 greased 9 by 5 inch loaf pans./ In a 300-325° F. oven, bake cakes for one hour./ Cool in pans./

Cheesecake

1 cup graham crackers,
  crushed
3 eggs
1 cup sugar
1 lb. cream cheese, softened
  at room temperature
Salt
3 cups sour cream
2 tsp. vanilla

Line a 10 inch springform pan with cracker crumbs./ In a mixing bowl, beat eggs till light yellow./ Add sugar and continue beating till mixture is very pale and thick./ Add cream cheese and a pinch of salt and beat well./ Mix in sour cream and vanilla./ Pour mixture into pan and sprinkle top around edges only with cracker crumbs./ In a 350° F. oven, bake for 45 to 50 minutes./ Do not open oven door during baking./ Then turn off oven, open door, and let cake sit in oven for one hour./ Remove to counter top and let sit for 30 minutes more./ Refrigerate until serving time./

Marble Cake

1 cup butter
1 cup sugar
4 eggs
3 cups sifted cake flour
3½ tsp. baking powder
½ tsp. salt
1 cup milk
1 tsp. vanilla extract
½ tsp. almond extract
1 cup chocolate syrup

In a mixing bowl, cream butter and sugar./ Add eggs./ Sift together flour, baking powder, and salt./ Mix together milk, vanilla and almond extract./ Add flour and milk mixtures alternately to first mixture, beating well./ Divide batter in half, and add chocolate syrup to one half./ Drop batter halves alternately by large spoonfuls into a large, well greased and floured tube pan./ In a 350°F. oven, bake cake for one hour./

Coffee Cake

¾ cup chopped nuts
½ cup brown sugar
1 tsp. cinnamon
½ cup butter
1 cup sugar
2 eggs
1 cup sour cream
2 cups flour
1 tsp. baking powder
1 tsp. baking soda
¼ tsp. salt
Vanilla (optional)

Mix together chopped nuts, brown sugar, and cinnamon, and set aside./ In a mixing bowl, cream butter and sugar./ Add eggs and beat well./ Blend in sour cream./ Sift together flour, baking powder, baking soda, and salt./ Add dry ingredients and vanilla, if desired, and mix well./

Pour half the batter into a greased tube pan./ Sprinkle half the nut mixture over the batter./ Add rest of batter, and top with remaining nut mixture./ In a 350° F. oven, bake cake for 40 to 45 minutes./

Sour Cream Blueberry Cake

½ cup butter, soft (or
  margarine)
1 cup sugar
3 eggs
2 cups sifted all-purpose
  flour
1 tsp. baking soda
1 tsp. baking powder
½ tsp. salt
1 cup sour cream
1 tsp. vanilla extract
1 tsp. ground cardamon
  (optional)
2 cups blueberries, washed
  and drained
½ cup brown sugar

In a mixing bowl, cream butter and sugar./ Add eggs to mixture, one at a time, beating well after each addition./ Sift flour, baking soda, baking powder, and salt together./ Gradually add dry ingredients to egg mixture, alternately with sour cream, ending with flour mixture, and combining thoroughly after each addition./ Stir vanilla, and cardamom, if desired, into batter./

Fold one cup blueberries into batter./ Pour half the batter into a well greased and floured 9 by 13 by 2 inch pan./ Cover batter with remaining blueberries and sprinkle with brown sugar./ Pour remaining batter on top./

In a 325° F. oven bake cake for 45 to 50 minutes, or until cake tests done./ Cool in pan 10 minutes./ To serve, cut cake and top servings with whipped cream./

Apple Cake

2 cups flour
2 cups plus 5 tbls. sugar
1 cup oil
4 eggs
¼ cup orange juice
1 tbls. baking powder
2½ tsp. vanilla extract
5 apples, sliced
2 tsp. cinnamon

In a large bowl, blend together well, flour, 2 cups sugar, oil, eggs, orange juice, baking powder, and vanilla./ In a separate bowl, mix together sliced apples, 5 tablespoons sugar, and cinnamon./

Pour half the batter into an ungreased tube pan, covering it with half the apple mixture./ Repeat the layers with remaining batter and apples./ In a 350° F. oven, bake for one hour and 15 minutes./ Let cake cool one hour before serving./

Ukranian Cheesecake

1 lb. farmer cheese
1 lb. cream cheese
2 cups sour cream
½ lb. confectioners' sugar
½ cup butter
3 tbls. cornstarch
3 tbls. flour
½ vanilla bean, finely
  chopped
4 eggs, separated
Juice of ½ lemon

Have all ingredients at room temperature./ In a mixing bowl, combine farmer cheese and cream cheese and mix together well for approximately 15 minutes./ Add sour cream, butter and half of the sugar and mix well./ Add cornstarch, flour and vanilla bean to mixture./ In a separate bowl, beat egg yolks with remaining sugar until light and fluffy./ Fold into cheese mixture./ Add lemon juice./ Beat egg whites until stiff and fold into mixture./ Pour batter into a greased 9 inch springform pan./ In a 325° F. oven, bake for 2 hours./ Do not open oven door during first hour of baking./ Allow cake to cool in open oven with heat turned off for one hour before removing./

Banana Cake Loaf

2 cups flour
1 tsp. baking soda
1 tsp. baking powder
2 to 3 large ripe bananas,
  mashed
1 cup sugar
1 cup walnuts, chopped (or
  Brazil nuts)
½ cup margarine, melted
½ cup raisins or currants or a
  combination of both
2 eggs

Into a mixing bowl, sift together flour, baking soda and baking powder./ Add bananas, sugar, walnuts, margarine, raisins and eggs and mix well./ Pour mixture into a greased and floured 9 by 5 inch loaf pan./ In a 350°F. oven, bake for one hour.

Grandma's Apple Cake

½ cup shortening (butter
   and/or margarine are best)
1¾ cup sugar
2 eggs
2¼ cups and 1 tbls. flour
2 tsp. baking powder
Rind of one lemon or orange,
   grated, or 1 tsp. vanilla for
   flavoring
5 medium apples, sliced
1 tsp. cinnamon
Raisins
Chopped nuts

In a bowl, cream shortening with ¾ cup sugar./ Add eggs and beat well./ Add 2¼ cups flour, baking powder and chosen flavoring, forming a soft dough./ Refrigerate for several hours./ Divide dough into 3 equal parts, then roll each third to fit an 8 or 9 inch square pan./

Combine sliced apples with one cup sugar, one tablespoon flour, cinnamon and raisins and nuts to taste./ Press ⅓ of dough into pan, top with half of apple filling./ Repeat layers, ending with dough./ Prick top layer of dough with fork to allow steam to escape./ Sprinkle with sugar, if desired./ In a 350° F. oven, bake apple cake for approximately one hour./

Aunt Marie's Easy Chocolate Cake

3 cups flour
2 cups sugar
⅔ cup cocoa
2 tsp. baking soda
1 tsp. salt
2 cups water
⅔ cup vegetable oil
2 tsp. vanilla extract
2 tsp. vinegar

Combine flour, sugar, cocoa, baking soda, and salt./ Add water, oil, vanilla, and vinegar, and mix well./ Pour batter into two 9 inch layer pans or a 9 by 13 inch pan./ In a 350°F. oven, bake cake for 25 to 30 minutes./

Dorothea's Whiskey Cake

1 box commercial Butter
   Recipe Golden cake mix
4 eggs
1 cup milk
1 small box vanilla instant
   pudding
½ cup corn oil
1 shot glass (1½ oz.) + ½
   cup whiskey
1 cup chopped nuts
1 cup sugar
½ cup butter

In a bowl combine cake mix, eggs, milk, pudding mix, oil, and one shot of whiskey./ Beat batter with an electric mixer for 5 minutes./ Fold in chopped nuts./ Pour batter into greased and floured Bundt pan./ In a 350° F. oven, bake cake for 60 minutes./

Meanwhile, in the top of a double boiler over hot water combine sugar, butter, and ½ cup whiskey and heat until melted together./ Pour half the mixture over cake, in pan, when cake is done and still hot./ Pour remaining topping over cake after it has cooled for 25 minutes./

Chocolate-Sundae Cake

3-¼ lb. bars sweet
 cooking chocolate
3 tbls. water
3 tbls. light cream
4½ cups sifted all-purpose
 flour
4½ tsp. double-acting
 baking powder
1½ tsp. salt
¾ cup butter (or margarine)
¾ cup + 2 tsp. soft
 vegetable shortening
2¼ cups sugar
6 eggs
1½ cups milk
1½ tsp. vanilla extract

In the top of a double boiler, over hot but not boiling water, melt 1½ bars of chocolate with water, stirring occasionally until smooth./ Remove chocolate from heat, and blend in cream./ Sift flour with baking powder and salt./

In large bowl, using electric mixer at medium speed, cream butter with ¾ cup shortening./ Gradually add sugar, beating approximately 5 minutes, until mixture is light and fluffy./ Beat in eggs, one at a time, beating one minute after each addition./

Combine milk and vanilla./ With mixer at low speed, add dry ingredients alternately with milk, starting and ending with flour, and beating thoroughly after each addition./ Batter will be thick./

Turn approximately ¼ of the batter into a 10-inch tube pan with greased and floured bottom only./ Drizzle batter with ⅓ of the melted chocolate mixture./ Repeat process, making 2 additional alternating layers of batter and chocolate./ Top with remaining batter./

In a 350° F. oven, bake cake for 70 to 80 minutes, or until cake tester inserted in center comes out clean./ Cool in pan 15 minutes, then turn out onto wire rack./ (A crack on the top of the cake is normal.)/

To make chocolate glaze, in the top of a double boiler over hot water, melt remaining 1½ bars of chocolate with 2 teaspoons shortening./ Stir until smooth./ Spoon glaze along top edge of cooled cake, letting it run over the sides./

Tomato Soup Cake

1 cup sugar
½ cup butter
2 eggs
1 tsp. cinnamon
½ tsp. ground cloves
½ tsp. nutmeg
2 cups flour
1 tsp. baking soda
¼ tsp. salt
1-10½ oz. can tomato soup
1 cup raisins
½ cup chopped walnuts

Cream sugar, butter, eggs, cinnamon, cloves, and nutmeg./ Sift together flour, baking soda, and salt./ Add dry ingredients to creamed mixture./ Add soup and mix well./ Blend raisins and nuts into batter./ Pour batter into greased tube pan, and bake cake in a 350° F. oven for 35 to 45 minutes./ Frost cooled cake with cream cheese icing./ Cake tastes best when prepared a day in advance of serving./

Grasshopper Cake

4 squares (4 oz.)
  unsweetened chocolate
½ cup boiling water
1¾ cup sugar
2¼ cups cake flour, sifted
3 tsp. baking powder
1 tsp. salt
½ cup oil
7 eggs, separated
¾ cup cold water
1 tsp. vanilla
½ tsp. cream of tartar

In a small saucepan over low heat, thoroughly blend chocolate, boiling water and ¼ cup sugar until chocolate is melted./ Cool mixture./ In a large bowl, sift together flour, 1½ cups sugar, baking powder and salt./ Make a well in center of dry ingredients and add, *in order given*, oil, egg yolks, cold water and vanilla./ Beat until very smooth./ Stir chocolate mixture into egg yolk mixture./ In another large bowl, beat egg whites with cream of tartar until stiff peaks form./ Pour chocolate batter in thin stream over entire surface of egg whites, then fold in./ Turn batter into an ungreased 10 inch tube pan./ In a 325° F. oven, bake for one hour and 5 minutes or until cake tests done./ Invert pan, cool thoroughly./

Grasshopper Filling

1 envelope unflavored
  gelatin
¼ cup cold water
½ cup green creme de
  menthe
⅓ cup white creme de cacao
2 cups heavy cream

In a small dish, soften gelatin in cold water./ In a saucepan, heat creme de menthe and creme de cacao./ Add softened gelatin, stirring, until gelatin is dissolved./ Cool mixture./ In a mixing bowl, whip heavy cream, then fold in gelatin mixture./ Refrigerate 15 minutes./

Split cooled cake into three layers./ Spread whipped cream filling between layers and on top of cake./ Refrigerate until serving time./

Blueberry Apple Crisp

1 cup flour
¾ cup sugar
1 egg
1 tsp. baking powder
¾ tsp. salt
3 cups blueberries
3 cups tart apples
2 tbls. brown sugar
⅓ cup butter
1 tsp. cinnamon

In a bowl, mix flour, sugar, egg, baking powder and salt together with a fork until crumbly./ In a separate bowl, combine blueberries, apples and brown sugar./ (Add more sugar if apples are very tart.)/ Spread fruit mixture in a greased baking dish./ Sprinkle dough crumbs on top./ Dot with butter and sprinkle cinnamon over all./ In a 375° F. oven, bake for 30 minutes./

Rolled Cake

3 cups flour
1 cup sugar
1 tsp. baking powder (full
  spoon)
½ cup margarine, softened
3 eggs
¼ cup orange juice
1 tsp. vanilla extract
Jam
Chopped nuts
Raisins
Sugar
Cinnamon

Into a mixing bowl, sift flour, sugar and baking powder together./ Cut margarine into pieces, add to flour mixture and rub mixture between hands until crumbly./ In a separate bowl, beat eggs lightly, add orange juice and vanilla, then mix into flour mixture until all liquid is absorbed./ If necessary, knead dough with more flour until it can be rolled./

Divide dough into 3 or 4 parts and roll each part out, not too thinly./ Spread with any kind of jam./ Combine nuts, raisins, sugar and cinnamon and sprinkle on top./ Roll dough up like a jelly roll./ Sprinkle with additional sugar and cinnamon./ Place rolled cakes on a greased cookie pan./ In a 375°F. oven, bake for 35 minutes, or until golden./

Orange Fluff Cake

6 eggs, separated
1½ cups sifted flour
⅓ cup oil
⅓ cup orange juice
2 tsp. baking powder
1 tsp. lemon juice
½ tsp. cream of tartar
½ cup sugar

In a bowl, mix thoroughly, egg yolks, flour, oil, orange juice, baking powder, and lemon juice./ In another bowl, beat egg whites with cream of tartar, gradually adding sugar, until stiff peaks form./ Fold egg whites into first mixture./ Pour batter into ungreased angel food pan./ In a 350° F. oven, bake for 35 minutes./ Let cake cool in pan 10 to 15 minutes, then remove to wire rack./ Frost cooled cake if desired./

Pineapple Cake

½ cup sweet butter
2 cups flour
1 cup sugar
2 tsp. baking powder
Salt
1-9 oz. can crushed
  pineapple
2 eggs, separated

In a mixing bowl, combine butter, flour, sugar, baking powder, and a pinch of salt, and rub ingredients together between hands until mixture is crumbly./ Set aside 2 tablespoons of mixture./ Add pineapple and egg yolks to mixing bowl./ Beat egg whites until stiff, and fold into batter./

Pour batter into an 8 by 8 inch greased and floured pan./ Sprinkle crumbs set aside over batter./ In a 350° F. oven, bake pineapple cake for 40 to 45 minutes./

Dutch Plum Cake

1 cup sifted flour
Sugar
½ tsp. baking powder
4 tbls. butter
1 egg
3 tbls. milk
2 tbls. flour
½ tsp. cinnamon
1½ lbs. (approx. 20) Italian
   prune plums

Sift one cup flour, 2 tablespoons sugar, and baking powder into a medium sized bowl./ Cut butter into dry ingredients./ In a small bowl, beat egg and milk together and stir into first mixture until well blended./ Spread dough evenly over the bottom and about halfway up the sides of a greased 9 inch round cake pan./

To make topping, combine ¼ to ½ cup sugar (determining quantity in proportion to tartness of plums) with 2 tablespoons flour and cinnamon./ Sprinkle 2 tablespoons of this mixture over dough in cake pan./ Wash and pit plums./ Arrange plums close together in a single layer, covering top of dough./ Plums will shrink as they bake./ Sprinkle plums with remaining sugar mixture./

In a 375° F. oven, bake cake for 40 minutes, or until plums are soft and crust is golden./

Passover Brownies

¼ cup vegetable shortening
1 cup sugar
2 eggs
½ cup cake meal
4 tbls. cocoa
⅛ tsp. salt
¼ cup milk
½ cup chopped nuts

In a bowl, cream shortening, add sugar./ Add eggs and mix well./ Sift cake meal, cocoa and salt together./ Add dry ingredients alternately with milk to shortening mixture./ Fold in chopped nuts./ In a greased square pan, in a 350° F. oven, bake brownies for 25 minutes./

Cherry Coconut Bars

1¼ cup flour
½ cup butter
3 tbls. confectioners' sugar
2 eggs, beaten
1 cup sugar
¾ cup chopped nuts
½ cup shredded coconut
½ cup Maraschino cherries,
   quartered
1 tsp. vanilla
½ tsp. baking powder
¼ tsp. salt

In a bowl, mix together one cup flour, butter and confectioners' sugar./ Spread batter in an ungreased 8 inch square pan./ In a 350°F. oven, bake for 25 minutes./

Into beaten eggs, stir ¼ cup flour, sugar, nuts, coconut, cherries, vanilla, baking powder and salt./ Spread mixture over baked crust and continue baking for 25 to 35 minutes./ Cut into small bars for serving./

Rugelahs

1 cup flour
½ cup sweet butter, softened
to room temperature
¼ lb. cream cheese,
softened to room
temperature
Sugar
Cinnamon
Chopped nuts
Raisins (optional)
Jam

In a bowl, cream butter, cream cheese and flour, forming a dough./ Cover tightly with wax paper and refrigerate overnight./ The next day, divide dough into thirds, then roll each third out into a circle./ Spread each dough circle with jam and sprinkle with any desired mixture of sugar, cinnamon, nuts and raisins./ Cut into pie wedges, then roll each wedge up from the outside in./ Shape into crescents./ In an ungreased shallow baking dish, in a 375° F. oven, bake rugelahs for 30 minutes./

Taiglach

1½ cups flour
3 eggs
1 tbls. oil
Chopped walnuts
1 lb. honey
1 cup sugar
1 tsp. powdered ginger
⅓ cup boiling water

Sift flour into a bowl./ Make a well in the center and drop in the eggs and oil./ Mix well with a fork until all the flour is absorbed into the dough mixture.

Pinch off pieces of dough and roll between hands, forming ropes ½ inch thick./ Cut ropes into ½ or ¾ inch pieces./ Stuff each piece of dough with a small piece of nut and roll into a ball./

In a heavy, broad-bottomed pan, bring honey and sugar to a rapid boil./ Drop all the dough pieces into boiling liquid a few pieces at a time (to keep the temperature from dropping)./ Cover pot, stir occasionally, and cook for 30 minutes./ When taiglach begin to brown, add ginger./ When taiglach are brown, remove from heat and add boiling water, stirring with a wooden spoon./ Using same spoon, remove taiglach from pan, place in a bowl and sprinkle with chopped nuts./

Fruit Squares

1 cup margarine, softened
3 cups flour
2 cups sugar
4 eggs
½ tsp. vanilla
½ tsp. almond extract
1 can pie filling

Mix first 6 ingredients together./ Spread ¾ of the dough onto a cookie pan with sides and top with pie filling./ Drop balance of dough by spoonfuls over filling./ In a 350° F. oven, bake for ½ hour./ Cut into squares for serving./

Dobosh Torte

1-6 oz. package chocolate
  bits
¼ cup boiling water or
  coffee
4 egg yolks
½ cup soft butter or
  margarine
¼ cup confectioners' sugar
2 tbls. rum flavoring
1 pound cake

Place chocolate pieces in blender with boiling water or coffee and blend on high speed for 6 seconds./ Add egg yolks, butter, sugar and rum flavoring and blend for 15 seconds longer or until smooth./ Chill frosting until it thickens to spreading consistency./

With a serrated knife, slice pound cake in 6 thin layers./ Frost cake with French butter cream between each layer and on top and sides./ Store torte in refrigerator where it will remain fresh for days./

Blueberry Torte

1¼ cups flour
½ cup plus 2 tsp. sugar
⅛ tsp. salt
Nutmeg
3 tbls. butter
2 tbls. vegetable shortening
3 eggs, separated
5 to 6 tbls. ice water
Rind of 2 lemons, grated
3 tbls. quick-cooking tapioca
2 tbls. lemon juice
½ tsp. cinnamon
4 cups blueberries
⅓ cup confectioners' sugar
⅛ tsp. cream of tartar

In a bowl, mix together flour, 2 teaspoons sugar, salt, and a sprinkle of nutmeg./ Cut in butter and shortening with 2 knives or a pastry blender until mixture resembles coarse cornmeal./ Mix 2 egg yolks with ice water, and stir into the flour mixture to make a very stiff dough./ With the back of a spoon, spread dough evenly in a greased 9 inch springform pan./ Refrigerate ½ hour./

Mix lemon rind with ½ cup sugar, tapioca, lemon juice, and cinnamon./ Toss mixture with blueberries until they are evenly coated./ Pour into torte shell and cover with silver foil./ In a 425° F. oven bake torte for 25 minutes./

Beat together 3 egg whites, confectioners' sugar, and cream of tartar until glossy and stiff./ Place meringue on top of baked torte./ In a 350° F. oven bake torte an additional 10 to 15 minutes, or until meringue is lightly browned./

Kay's Old Fashioned Sugar Cookies

½ cup butter
1 cup sugar
1 egg, well beaten
2 tbls. milk
¼ tsp. salt
1 tsp. vanilla
2 cups flour, sifted
2 tsp. baking powder

In a bowl, mix ingredients together in order given above./ Refrigerate dough for easier handling./ Cut out cookies and place on an ungreased cookie sheet./ In a 350° F. oven, bake for 8 to 12 minutes./ Remove cookies from sheet immediately./

Black Walnut Cookies

1 cup brown sugar
½ cup shortening
1 egg, beaten
1 tsp. vanilla
1½ cups flour
½ tsp. baking soda
½ tsp. salt
1 cup chopped black walnuts

Frosting
¼ cup maple syrup
¼ cup butter
½ tsp. maple flavoring
2½ cups confectioners' sugar

In a bowl, cream sugar and shortening until light and creamy./ Beat in egg and vanilla./ Sift together flour, baking soda and salt and stir into sugar mixture./ Stir in black walnuts./ Drop by teaspoonfuls onto a greased baking sheet and bake in a 350° F. oven for 12 to 15 minutes./ When cool, frost tops of cookies./

Heat syrup, add butter and stir until melted./ Stir in flavoring./ Add enough confectioners' sugar to bring mixture to a spreading consistency./

Funnel Cakes ("Birds Nests")

Salad oil
1 cup and 2 tbls. flour
¾ cup milk
1 egg, beaten
1 tsp. baking powder
Salt
Confectioners' sugar

In a large skillet, heat salad oil to 370°F., about ¾ inch deep./ Whisk together flour, milk, egg, baking powder and a dash of salt./ Using a double plastic bag with one corner cut to make a ½ inch spout, pour about ¼ cup batter into bag./ Allow batter to run out into hot oil while making a spiral about 6 inches in diameter./ Fry approximately 5 to 6 minutes, turning once, until golden brown./ Drain on paper towels./ Repeat process with remaining batter, stirring batter each time./ Sprinkle cooked cakes with confectioner's sugar and serve warm with tea or coffee, as a garnish with ice cream or fruit or with syrup alone./ Funnel cakes will stay fresh, unsugared, in a tightly covered container for about 2 weeks./ Sugar just before serving./ (Batter can be made up to 2 weeks before using if refrigerated.)/

Danish Butter Cookies

1 cup butter
1 cup sugar
1 egg, beaten
2 cups flour
½ tsp. cream of tartar
½ tsp. baking soda
Salt
1 tsp. lemon extract

In a bowl, cream shortening./ Add sugar and beaten egg./ Sift in dry ingredients, a little at a time./ Add lemon extract to mixture./ Roll dough into small balls and press down with a fork dipped in flour to form crisscross pattern./ Place on a cookie sheet and bake in a 350°F. oven for 12 to 15 minutes, until cookie edges are brown./

Pennsylvania Dutch Cake

1½ cups boiling water
1 cup oatmeal
½ tsp. salt
½ cup butter
1 cup sugar
1 cup light brown sugar
2 eggs
1½ cups flour
1 cup chopped nuts
1 tsp. cinnamon
1 tsp. baking soda

Cook oatmeal and salt in boiling water, then let cool./ In a mixing bowl, cream butter, sugar, and brown sugar./ Add eggs and oatmeal to sugar mixture, and mix well./ Add flour, nuts, cinnamon, and baking soda, and blend batter./ Pour batter into two 9 inch layer pans or one large pan./ In a 350°F. oven, bake cake for 45 minutes./

Topping
6 tbls. butter
1 cup shredded coconut
1 cup chopped nuts
¾ cup light brown sugar
1 tsp. vanilla extract

Melt butter./ Blend butter with coconut, nuts, brown sugar, and vanilla, and mix well./ Spread topping over cake when cool./

Date And Chocolate Bits Cake

1½ cups boiling water
1 cup dates, chopped
2¼ tsp. baking soda
1¼ cups sugar
¾ cup soft vegetable
   shortening
2 eggs
1¾ cups flour
½ tsp. salt
1-6 oz. package semi-sweet
   chocolate chips
½ to 1 cup chopped nuts

Combine boiling water, dates, and 1½ teaspoons baking soda./ Let mixture cool for one hour./
Cream one cup sugar and vegetable shortening./ Add eggs and beat well./ Blend in date mixture thoroughly./ Sift together flour, ¾ teaspoon baking soda, and salt, and add to batter, beating well./ Pour batter into a greased and floured 9 by 13½ inch pan./ Spread chocolate chips over top, especially into edges./ Sprinkle ¼ cup sugar over the chocolate chips, and then cover entire cake surface with chopped nuts./ In a 350°F. oven, bake cake for 35 to 45 minutes, or until toothpick inserted in center comes out clean./

Hot Water Sponge Cake

4 large eggs, separated
½ tsp. salt
2 tsp. cold water
½ cup hot water
1½ cups sugar
1 tsp. vanilla
1½ cups sifted cake flour
1 tsp. cream of tartar

In the top of a double boiler, beat egg yolks with ¼ teaspoon salt./ Add cold water and beat well./ Add hot water to mixture, place pot over hot water, and heat until frothy and bubbly, and greatly increased in volume./ Remove from heat and add sugar and vanilla to the mixture, and beat well./ Fold flour into batter./

Beat egg whites with cream of tartar and ¼ teaspoon salt until stiff./ Fold egg white mixture into batter./ Pour batter into an ungreased angel food cake pan./ In a 325° F. oven, bake sponge cake for 45 minutes./

Pineapple Egg Sponge Cake

6 eggs, separated, at room
temperature
1½ cups sugar
½ tsp. salt
½ cup unsweetened
pineapple juice
Rind of ½ lemon, grated
¼ tsp. cream of tartar
1½ cups cake flour

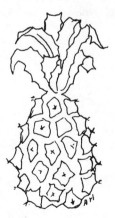

Beat egg yolks until thick and lemon colored./ Add ¾ cup sugar and the salt to yolks, and beat mixture until it is thoroughly blended and very pale./ Add pineapple juice and lemon rind and continue beating until light and thick./

In a separate bowl, beat egg whites until frothy./ Add remaining ¾ cup sugar and cream of tartar and beat until high, thick, and shining./ Fold cake flour into egg white mixture./

Fold egg *yolk* mixture into egg *white* mixture./ Pour batter into ungreased 10 inch tube pan./ Bake cake as follows, to assure slow rising./ (To prevent cake's falling, do not open oven door while baking.)/ Oven should be preheated to 250° F./

Bake cake at 250° F. for 5 minutes;
                275° F. for 5 minutes;
                300° F. for 5 minutes; and
                325° F. for 45 minutes.

Invert tube pan over soda bottle to cool cake./ When cool, turn right side up and gently release cake from sides of pan using a spatula./ Cover top of pan with metal tray and turn cake out, giving the tray a hard tap on the table to release cake completely and cleanly from tube pan./

Black Russian Cake

1-18½ oz. box deep
  chocolate cake mix
¾ cup + 2 tbls. strong
  coffee
4 eggs, room temperature
1-4½ oz. package instant
  chocolate pudding
½ cup combined Kahlua and
  crème de cacao
6 tbls. vegetable oil
1 cup sifted confectioners'
  sugar
2 tbls. Kahlua
2 tbls. crème de cacao

In a large mixing bowl, combine cake mix, ¾ cup coffee, eggs, pudding mix, Kahlua and creme de cacao mixture, and oil./ With electric mixer at medium speed, beat batter for 4 minutes, or until smooth./

Spoon batter into a well greased Bundt pan./ In a 350° F. oven, bake cake for 45 to 50 minutes./ Remove cake from pan when cool./ Make topping by combining sugar, Kahlua, creme de cacao, and 2 tablespoons coffee, and mixing well./ Punch holes in cake with cake tester or meat fork./ Spoon topping over cake./

Chocolate Whipped Cream Cake

2 cups sifted cake flour
1⅔ cups sugar
5 tbls. cocoa
4 tsp. baking powder
1 tsp. salt
1⅓ cups diluted evaporated
  milk (half water)
⅔ cup soft shortening
1⅓ tsp. vanilla extract
3 eggs
2 cups heavy cream
3 tsp. confectioners' sugar
1½ tsp. almond flavoring

Sift together flour, sugar, cocoa, baking powder, and salt./ Add diluted evaporated milk, shortening, and vanilla, to dry ingredients, and beat mixture 2 minutes./ Add eggs to batter, and beat 2 additional minutes./ Pour batter into 2 greased and floured 9 inch pans, and bake in moderate oven (350°F.) for 30 to 40 minutes./

To make filling for cake, beat heavy cream with confectioners' sugar and almond flavoring./ Split cooled cake layers, and spread whipped filling between all 4 layers./ Frost cake with milk chocolate icing./

Milk Chocolate Icing
½ cup cocoa
5 tbls. shortening
2⅔ cups confectioners' sugar
7 tbls. evaporated milk
1⅓ tsp. vanilla extract

Melt cocoa and shortening together./ Remove from heat and stir in confectioners' sugar, evaporated milk, and vanilla./ Place mixture in a bowl set in a pan of ice and water and beat with a wooden spoon until icing is thick enough to spread and hold its shape./

House of Lyons Restaurant

Keks (Fruit Cake)

1 cup sugar
4 eggs
1 cup butter, melted and
  cooled
½ cup sour cream
1 tsp. lemon extract
Salt
1½ cups glazed cherries,
  chopped
1¼ cups raisins
2¾ cups flour
2 tsp. baking powder
½ cup heavy cream

In a bowl, beat sugar and eggs together until light and foamy./ Add butter, sour cream, lemon extract and a pinch of salt and mix well./ Coat chopped cherries and raisins with a little flour and gradually add to mixture./ Combine 2¾ cups flour with baking powder and add to mixture alternately with heavy cream./ Pour into a greased and floured loaf pan./ In a 350 to 375° F. oven, bake cake for approximately one hour, or until toothpick inserted in center comes out clean./

Stevensville Country Club Hotel

Mary Mellan's Apricot Cake

3 cups flour
1 cup butter
1½ cups sugar
3 tbls. lemon juice (juice of
  one large lemon)
Rind of large lemon, grated
6 eggs
1 heaping tsp. baking powder
Salt
2 jars apricot jam
12 oz. chopped walnuts

With a pastry blender, mix together flour, butter, ½ cup sugar, lemon juice, lemon rind, 2 eggs, baking powder, and a pinch of salt./ Place ⅔ of the dough around the sides and bottoms of 2 greased 7 by 11 inch cake pans./ Roll our remaining dough and cut it into ½ inch strips with pastry cutter./ Place cut strips in refrigerator./

Separate 4 eggs, and beat egg whites and yolks separately./ Add one cup sugar and walnuts to beaten yolks./ Spread jam on dough in pans./ Fold beaten egg whites into egg yolk and sugar mixture, and spread over apricot jam layer./ Lattice top of filling with strips of dough./ In a 350° F. oven, bake apricot cake for 35 minutes./

Chocolate Ice Box Cake

3-4 oz. bars sweet
  cooking chocolate
3 tsp. hot brewed coffee
6 eggs, separated
1 tsp. vanilla extract
3 boxes tea biscuits
1 cup whipping cream
Maraschino cherries

Melt chocolate in top of double boiler./ Remove chocolate from heat, and blend in hot coffee./ Beat egg yolks, one at a time, into chocolate mixture./ Beat egg whites until stiff but not dry, and fold them in./ Add vanilla./

Line a 9 inch square pan with wax paper./ Alternate layers of biscuits and chocolate filling five times, ending with a chocolate layer./ Allow cake to stand to allow chocolate to soak through layers./ Refrigerate cake at least 6 hours./ Whip cream./ Serve cake garnished with whipped cream and maraschino cherries./

Lottie's Kolachki Cookies

1 cake yeast
4 cups flour, sifted
Rind of one lemon, grated
1 cup sweet butter
6 egg yolks
1 cup heavy cream
½ lb. walnuts, chopped
½ cup sugar
1 tsp. milk
Confectioners' sugar

Into a mixing bowl, work yeast through sieve with fingers./ Add flour and lemon rind and mix well./ Cut in butter with pastry blender./ Beat egg yolks with heavy cream and add to mixture./ Refrigerate dough overnight./

Mix together walnuts, sugar and enough milk, approximately one teaspoon, to bind mixture together./ Divide dough into 4 parts, and roll out on confectioners' sugar./ Cut into 2 inch squares./ Pile each square with a teaspoon of walnut filling and roll lightly./ Roll again in confectioners' sugar./ On a greased cookie sheet, bake in 350°F. oven for 15 minutes./

Beverages

Blackberry Wine (Bramble)

Yield: 4 quarts

3 lbs. blackberries
1 gallon boiling water
3 lbs. granulated sugar

Wash blackberries well, and drain./ Place berries in a large bowl, and add boiling water./ Stir mixture well, cover bowl, and let stand for 10 days./ Strain juice through damp muslin./ Add sugar to strained juice, and stir mixture well./ Cover and let stand for 3 days, stirring daily./

Bottle wine, and cork loosely for 10 days./ Wine is ready to drink in 6 months./

Plum Wine

Yield: 6 quarts

3½ lbs. ripe plums
1 lb. raisins
1 orange, cut in small pieces
1 lemon, cut in small pieces
1 gallon boiling water
4 lbs. sugar
1 cake yeast

Wash, drain, and pit plums./ Place plums, raisins, orange and lemon in a large bowl, and pour boiling water over fruit./ Mash the mixture, and stir it with wooden spoon./ Cover bowl, and let stand for 10 days./

Remove mold carefully, trying not to break into the liquid./ Strain liquid into another bowl./ Add sugar and yeast to the juice, and stir until sugar is dissolved./ Cover bowl, and stir daily for 3 days./ Bottle the wine, corking it loosely for 10 days./ Wine is ready for drinking in 6 months./

Fruit Punch

Yield: 30 cups

2 cups sugar
1 cup water
2 cups strawberry syrup
1 cup tea
Juice of 5 oranges
Juice of 5 lemons
1 can crushed pineapple
Ice water
1 cup maraschino cherries
1 quart bottle ginger ale

In a saucepan, boil sugar and water together for 10 minutes./ Add strawberry syrup, tea, orange juice, lemon juice, and pineapple./ Let stand 30 minutes./ Strain mixture, and add enough ice water to make 1½ gallons of liquid./ Turn punch into a large punch bowl over a piece of ice./ Add cherries and ginger ale./

Dandelion Wine

Yield: 4 quarts

2½ quarts tightly packed dandelion blossoms that have been picked in full bloom at midday
4 quarts boiling water
3 lbs. sugar
1 lb. seedless raisins
1 orange
1 lemon
½ cake yeast

Wash blossoms well, and drain./ In a large container with cover, pour boiling water over dandelion blossoms, and let stand overnight./ The next morning, strain out blossoms and discard them./ Return liquid to container and add sugar./

Put raisins, orange, and lemon through a food chopper, and add to liquid./ Add yeast to mixture./ Cover and let stand at room temperature until thoroughly fermented, stirring mixture daily./ Do not leave near stove./

Strain fermented wine and bottle it./ Do not put corks in tightly for several days./ Use wine in the autumn./

Mulled Wine

Yield: 8 cups

2 sticks cinnamon
½ tsp. black peppercorns
½ tsp. cloves
2 bottles Burgundy wine
¼ cup sugar
1 cup kirsch brandy (or cognac)

Tie cinnamon, peppercorns, and cloves in a cheesecloth bag./ In a large pot, simmer spice bag, wine, and sugar for 4 to 5 minutes./ Add kirsch, and heat through./ Remove spice bag./ Pour mulled wine into heated mugs./

Fruit Wine

Yield: 3 to 4 quarts

8 lbs. grapes, cherries or raspberries
4 lbs. sugar
1 quart water

Wash fruit, remove stems and place in earthenware crock./ Add 2 pounds of sugar and cover with cheesecloth or other loosely woven cloth./ Let stand in warm place for one to 2 weeks, until fermentation is over./

In a large kettle, combine remaining 2 pounds of sugar with water and bring to a boil./ Let cool, then add to fruit./ Let mixture stand in cool place for one month./ Pour clear wine off the top and strain if necessary./ Store in glass wine bottles./

Cherry Liqueur

Yield: 1 quart

1 quart grain alcohol (or Vodka)
2 cups ripe chokeberries (wild cherries) or blackberries, crushed
½ lb. sugar

Mix together alcohol, crushed berries, and sugar, and pour mixture into wine bottle./ Leave bottle in the sun 6 to 8 weeks to distill./ Filter wine, and then pour into clean bottle./

Raisin Wine

Yield: 14 quarts

5 lbs. raisins
5 lbs. sugar
Water
3 packages yeast
Orange and lemon slices

In a large pot, cook raisins in water to cover for 30 minutes, then allow to cool./ Dissolve the sugar and yeast in water and add to raisins./ Pour mixture into a 5 gallon jug or ceramic container and fill with more water./ Add several orange and lemon slices, then cover with a clean cloth and loose lid./ Allow mixture to sit undisturbed in a cool dark place for several weeks, then drain off the raisins and citrus slices and allow to settle again for 3 to 4 weeks./ Bottle in gallon jugs, age 3 months and siphon into quart bottles for serving./

Chokeberry (Wild Cherry) Wine

Yield: 1 quart

Ripe chokeberries (wild cherries), crushed to yield 2 cups of juice
1 quart water
¾ lb. sugar

Pour chokeberry juice into a wide-mouthed bottle./ Add water and sugar./ Cover bottle top with piece of paper./ For two days, occasionally shake bottle briskly./ Then, ferment wine in a cool, undisturbed place, such as a basement, for 6 to 8 weeks./

After fermentation, carefully discard residue at bottle top with a silver spoon./ Pour clear wine into a clean wine bottle, and cork./ The older the wine, the better the taste./

Party Punch

Yield: approximately 20 cups

2 quarts water
3 cups orange juice
2 cups lemon juice
1½ cups grape juice
1½ cups sugar
Sherry (optional)
Orange slices
Grapefruit slices
Lemon slices

In a large container, mix together water, orange juice, lemon juice, grape juice, sugar and sherry./ Cover and refrigerate./ To serve, pour over a block of ice and float fruit slices on top./

Cooking Cues

Avocados: To inhibit darkening of avocado meat, return the pit to the vicinity of the meat./ If avocado is cut in half, close it back up around the pit; if the meat is in a bowl, place the pit in the bowl./ Sprinkling lemon or lime juice on the exposed meat is also effective./

Bacon: When broiling bacon or other meats on a rack, place a piece or two of dry bread in the broiler pan to soak up the fat./ This eliminates smoking of fat and reduces chances of fire./

Baking Powder: A workable substitution when a recipe calls for baking powder and you have none is to mix 2 teaspoons cream of tartar, 1 teaspoon baking soda and ½ teaspoon salt, for every one cup of flour in recipe./ This must be used immediately, however./ It won't be effective for more than a day or so./

To test for staleness in old baking powder, put one teaspoonful in a cup of hot water./ If it bubbles a lot, it's good./

Bread: To revitalize dried out bread, wrap in a damp towel and refrigerate for 24 hours./ Then remove the towel and heat the bread in a 350°F. oven for 5 minutes./

If bread is stale, it can be helped by either pouring ½ teaspoon of water on it, sealing in a brown paper bag and heating it in a 350°F. oven for 10 to 15 minutes, or plunging entire loaf or rolls into cold water for an instant, then baking on a cookie sheet in a 350°F. oven for 10 minutes./

When bread dough won't rise, additional heat helps./ You may set an electric heating pad on low, cover with tin foil and then place bowl of dough on foil, or place bowl of dough in dishwasher set for drying cycle./

Butter: If butter begins to brown too fast, add a small amount of any type of oil to the pan./ The flavor remains the same and the combination of the two doesn't burn as easily as butter alone./

If butter is hard to cream, slice it into a warmed bowl./

Cake: To give more of a homemade taste to a cake mix, add a teaspoon of vanilla./

If cake is too crumbly or soft to frost or cut, freeze it, then frost or slice, and then thaw./

Cake: If a cake is stuck to the baking pan, you may let it sit for 5 minutes, so that it will shrink a little and may be easier to remove./ Alternately, you may remove the pan from the oven and place in a damp cold cloth./

Cauliflower: Add a little lemon juice to cooking water to prevent discoloration while cooking./ To reduce cooking odors, change the water after the first 5 minutes of cooking or add a piece of bread, preferably rye, to the pot./

Chocolate: Three tablespoons of cocoa and one tablespoon of shortening may be substituted for one square of unsweetened chocolate./

A square or two of chocolate may be melted in a soup ladle for easy handling and pourability./

Clams: To open clams easily, drop them four at a time into boiling water./ After 15 seconds, remove and slip a knife between the shells./

Coconut: To open a coconut easily, bake it for 20 minutes at 300°F./ At the end of this time, it will have either opened itself or a light tap is all that's needed./

Crackers: To revitalize soggy crackers, place them on a cookie sheet and bake for 2 or 3 minutes at 350°F./

Cream: If you're out of whipping cream, you may slowly add baking soda to sour cream until it reaches the desired sweetness./ Start with a tiny pinch; a teaspoon per pint is the most you'd ever use./

Egg Whites: For a thicker meringue, add ½ cup of sugar to 3 egg whites at room temperature./

A pinch of baking soda helps when egg whites won't whip./

Egg whites will keep for several weeks in an airtight jar in the refrigerator./ Measure out what you need, ¼ cup equals 2 egg whites./

Freeze single egg whites in ice cube trays, then thaw and beat when needed./

Egg Yolks: To store for several days, place in an airtight jar, cover yolks with water and refrigerate./

Eggs: For easy cleaning of eggs dropped on the floor, cover with lots of salt and let stand for 20 minutes./ It should then sweep up easily with a broom./

To prevent boiled eggs from cracking while cooking, add one teaspoon of salt or a few drops of lemon juice or vinegar to the water./

Fat: To remove odors from frying fat or shortening that you'd like to reuse, fry potato slices in it until brown./

Fish: When raw fish or shrimp is too salty, adding 1 cup of vinegar per quart of liquid to cooking water helps cut down saltiness./

Freezing: When freezing a casserole dish, line it with tin foil before filling, then freeze./ When frozen solid, remove food wrapped in foil from dish, seal tightly and replace in freezer./ When ready to bake, slip food from foil back into dish and cook./

Tomato paste may be frozen by tablespoons on a tray and when frozen solid transferred to a plastic bag for easier storage./ Whipped cream may be frozen the same way./

Use plastic ice cube trays to freeze small amounts./ When frozen, remove cubes and store in plastic bags./

To prevent exposed flesh of fruit from darkening, coat with a little lemon juice./

Gelatin: To prepare gelatin in a hurry, add just enough hot water to the powder to dissolve it, a few tablespoons should be enough./ Then use ice water for the rest of the liquid./ Any fruits that are added should be very cold./

Greens: To rescue wilted salad greens, dip them in hot water, then in ice water with a dash of vinegar./ Shake excess water off them and chill in refrigerator for one hour./

Ham: If a ham is too salty, slice it and soak the slices in milk for 15 to 30 minutes, then wash them off with cold water./ This won't affect the taste of the ham except for making it less salty./

Icing: If icing is too thick, and it's already made, stir in some cream until it reaches the desired consistency./ If it gets too thick while being made, stir in a few drops of lemon juice or boiling water./

If icing won't thicken, beat in confectioners' sugar, a little at a time./ Beat vigorously, preferably near heat./

Jelly: If jelly won't thicken, place a grated carrot in a piece of cheesecloth and squeeze a few drops of carrot juice into the jelly./

Lemon: To revitalize a dried up, old lemon, boil it for about 5 minutes and it will become more juicy./ Or bake it for 5 minutes in a 300°F. oven./

Marshmallows: To prevent sticking when cutting marshmallows or chopping dates, dip scissors in water./

To freshen hard or stale marshmallows, seal them in an air-tight plastic bag for 3 days with a slice of fresh bread./

Mushrooms: Wipe mushrooms with a damp cloth, rub them with lemon juice and store in the refrigerator to prevent darkening./

Nuts: If almonds or similar nuts are hard to crack, drop the whole nut in boiling water, remove from the heat and let stand for 3 minutes./ For pecans and such, cover with boiling water and let stand until cold./ Crack them then with a nut-cracker end to end and the nut should come out whole./

Onions: To alleviate crying when peeling or slicing onions, chill onions in freezer for 10 to 15 minutes before slicing./ Or peel them under cold running water./

Oranges: When you need cleanly peeled, neat orange sections, pour boiling water over oranges and let them stand for 5 minutes./ The peel and white membranes will come off easily./ This process permanently loosens the peel so it can be done in advance and the oranges refrigerated with the peel still on./

Pancakes: To reuse cold, soggy pancakes, place them between the folds of a dish towel and reheat in a 250°F. oven./

Pasta: To prevent gummy noodles, rice, macaroni and spaghetti, add 2 tablespoons of cooking oil to water before boiling./

Pimentos: In a small jar, cover pimentos with vinegar and refrigerate, to retard spoilage./

Pineapple: To speed up a pineapple's ripening, seal it in a brown paper bag and store it in a warm, not hot, place./ When one of the center leaves pulls out easily, it's ripe./

Potatoes: Baked potatoes can be reheated without overcooking by dipping them in cold water, then placing in a 350° F. oven for 10 minutes./

Raisins: To prevent raisins from sticking to bottom when used in baking, place them in the top of a flour sifter before adding flour to the mixture, then add flour-coated raisins to batter./

If raisins are stuck together, heat them in a 300°F. oven for a few minutes and they will unstick themselves./

Rice: To rescue burned rice, turn off the heat, place the heel of a loaf of bread on top of the rice, cover the pot and let stand for 5 minutes./ All the scorched taste should go into the bread.

Roast Beef: For perfect rib roast, meat must be at room temperature./ After seasoning, place roast on rack in roasting pan./ Place in a preheated 500°F. oven and roast 15 minutes for each rib./ Turn off heat and leave in oven for 2 hours./ The same procedure may be followed with eye round roast with the only change being to roast it 5 minutes per pound./

Rolling Pin: If dough sticks and is difficult to roll out and you don't want to add more flour, place the rolling pin in the freezer until very cold./

Sauces: To correct for oversalting a sauce, soup, or a stew, add a couple of pinches of brown sugar./ It overcomes saltiness without noticeably sweetening./ Thin slices of raw potato may also be added and kept in the liquid until they become translucent./

Stews: To thicken a stew, add a handful of mashed-potato flakes and stir./

Sugar: To soften hard, lumpy sugar, you may push it through a sieve, steam it in the top of a double boiler or place it, in its bag, not box, in a 350°F. oven./ By the time the bag is warm, the sugar should be softened./

Tomatoes: For easier peeling of tomatoes, pour boiling water over them and let stand for 3 minutes./

Vegetables: To reduce smells when cooking vegetables, place a heel of bread on top./ This is good for broccoli, cabbage, brussel sprouts, etc./

To revitalize old vegetables, add a pinch of sugar and a pinch of salt for each cup of cooking liquid./

Whipped Cream: When cream won't whip even though chilled and all utensils are chilled, add either one unbeaten egg white, 3 or 4 drops of lemon juice, a pinch of gelatin powder or a sprinkle of salt and keep beating./

For most uses, a mashed banana beaten up with one stiffly beaten egg white and sugar to taste can be substituted for whipped cream./

Table of Equivalents

When You Need	You May Use . . . .
1 cup granulated sugar	1 cup firmly packed brown sugar
	¾ cup honey
	1½ cups molasses
	2 cups corn syrup
	1½ cups maple syrup
	(reduce other liquids in recipe
	accordingly)
1 cup corn syrup	1 cup granulated sugar and ¼ cup liquid
1 cup honey	1¼ cups sugar and ¼ cup liquid
1 cup cake flour	1 cup all-purpose flour less 2 tablespoons
1 teaspoon cornstarch	2 teaspoons flour
1 cup fresh milk	½ cup evaporated milk and ½ cup water
	4 tablespoons powdered whole milk
	and 1 cup water
	4 tablespoons powdered whole milk
	and 2 tablespoons butter and
	1 cup water
1 cup light cream	7/8 cup milk and 3 tablespoons butter
1 cup heavy cream	¾ cup milk and ⅓ cup butter
1 cup butter	1 cup and 2 tablespoons vegetable
	shortening
2-8″ layer pans	2 thin 8x8x2″ squares
	18 to 24-2½″ cupcakes
3-8″ layer pans	2-9x9x2″ squares
2-9″ layer pans	2-8x8x2″ squares
	3 thin 8″ layers
	15x10x1″ rectangle
	30-2½″ cupcakes
2-8x8x2″ squares	13x9x2″ rectangle
9x9x2″ square	2 thin 8″ layers
2-9x9x2″ squares	3-8″ layers
12x8x2″ rectangle	2-8″ layers
9x5x3″ loaf pan	9x9x2″ square
	24 to 30-2½″ cupcakes
8x4x3″ loaf pan	8x8x2″ square
9x3½″ tube pan	2-9″ layers
	24 to 30 2½″ cupcakes
10x4″ tube pan	2-9x5x3″ loaves
	13x9x2″ rectangle
	2-15x10x1″ rectangles

Arrowroot:

1 tsp.	1 tbls. flour
2 tsp.	1 tbls. cornstarch

Bay Leaf:

¼ tsp. cracked	1 whole bay leaf

Green Peppers:

1 tbls., rehydrated	3 tbls. chopped fresh green pepper

Red Peppers:

1 tbls., rehydrated	3 tbls. chopped fresh red pepper
1 tbls., rehydrated	2 tbls. chopped pimento

Chives: (see Onions, Shredded Green)

Cornstarch: (see Arrowroot)

Flour: (see Arrowroot)

Garlic Powder:

½ tsp.	1 medium-size clove garlic

Ginger:

1 tsp. whole (soak in cold water several hrs., then chop finely or grate)	2 tsp. chopped fresh ginger
2 tsp. crystallized, chopped or slivered (wash sugar from ginger or leave on if flavor is compatable)	1 tsp. chopped fresh ginger
¼ tsp. ground	1 tsp. chopped fresh ginger
¼ tsp. ground	2 tsp. chopped crystallized ginger

Horseradish:

1 tbls., rehydrated in 1 tbls. water and mixed with 1 tbls. vinegar and sugar and salt to taste	2 tbls. bottled prepared horseradish

Lemon Peel:

1 tsp.	1 tsp. grated fresh lemon peel
1 tsp.	½ tsp. lemon extract
1 tsp.	grated peel of 1 medium-size lemon

Mushrooms (Powdered):

1 tbls.	3 tbls. whole dried mushrooms
1 tbls.	4 oz. fresh or 2 oz. canned

Mustard:

1 tsp. Mild	1 tbls. mild prepared mustard
1 tsp. Hot	1 tbls. hot prepared mustard

Onion Powder:

1 tbls., rehydrated	1 medium-size onion, chopped
1 tbls., rehydrated	4 tbls. chopped onions

Onions (Instant Minced):

1 tbls., rehydrated	1 small onion, chopped
1 tbls., rehydrated	2 tbls. chopped onions
1 tbls., without rehydrating	1 tbls. Instant Toasted Onions

Onions (Shredded Green):

½ tsp.	2 tsp. finely chopped chives
½ tsp.	2 tsp. finely chopped green onion tops

Orange Peel:

1 tbls.	1 tbls. grated fresh orange peel
2 tsp.	1 tsp. orange extract
1 tbls.	grated peel of 1 medium-size orange

Parsley:

1 tsp.	1 tbls. chopped fresh parsley

Peppermint:

1 tbls.	¼ cup chopped fresh mint

Vanilla Beans:

1-inch piece	1 tsp. pure vanilla extract

Measurements
Before and After

Cereals:	Before	After
Cornmeal	1 cup	5½ cups cooked
Macaroni	3½ oz. (1 cup)	2 cups cooked
Noodles	4 oz. (3 cups)	3 cups cooked
Quick-cooking Oats	1 cup	1¾ cups cooked
Rice, long-grained	1 cup	3 cups cooked
Spaghetti	7 oz.	4 cups cooked

Bread and Crumbs:		
Bread, fresh	1½ slices	1 cup soft crumbs
	2 slices	1 cup small cubes
Bread, dry	1 slice	¼ cup fine dry crumbs
Chocolate wafers	19 wafers	1 cup crumbs
Graham crackers	14 square crackers	1 cup fine crumbs
Potato chips	4 oz.	2 cups coarsely crushed
Saltine crackers	28 crackers	1 cup finely crushed
Vanilla wafers	22 wafers	1 cup finely crushed
Zwieback	6 oz.	2 cups finely crushed

Dairy Products:		
Cheese	¼ lb.	1 cup grated or crumbled
Cheddar cheese	1 lb.	4 cups shredded
Eggs, hard-boiled	3 large	1 cup chopped
Whipping cream	1 cup	2 cups whipped

Fruit:		
Apples, whole	1 lb. (3 medium)	2¾ cups sliced
Bananas, whole	1 lb. (3 to 4)	1⅓ cups mashed
Grapes	1 lb.	2½ cups seeded
Lemon	1 medium	3 tbls. juice
		1 tsp. grated peel
Orange	1 medium	⅓ cup juice
		¾ cup diced
Peaches and pears	1 lb. (4 medium)	2 cups sliced
Rhubarb, cut	1 lb.	2 cups cooked
Strawberries	1 quart	4 cups sliced

Fresh Vegetables:	Before	After
Beans, green	1 lb. (3 cups)	2½ cups cooked
Cabbage	1 lb. (1 head)	4½ cups shredded
Carrots, without tops	1 lb.	3 cups shredded
		2½ cups diced
	1 large one	1 cup grated
Celery	3 ribs	1 cup chopped
Corn	12 medium ears	2½ cups cooked kernels
Green pepper	6 oz. (1 large)	1 cup diced
Lettuce	1 lb. (1 head)	6¼ cups torn
Mushrooms	8 oz. (3 cups)	1 cup sliced, cooked
Onions	1 medium	½ cup chopped
Peas	1 lb.	1 cup shelled
Potatoes	1 lb. (3 medium)	2 cups cubed, cooked
		1¾ cups mashed
		3 cups sliced, raw
Tomatoes	1 lb. (4 large)	2½ cups cooked

Nuts:		
Almonds	1 lb. (in shell)	1¼ cups shelled
	1 lb. (shelled)	3¼ cups chopped
Pecans	1 lb. (in shell)	2 cups shelled
	1 lb. (shelled)	4½ to 5 cups, halves
Walnuts	1 lb. (in shell)	1½ to 1¾ cups shelled
	1 lb. (shelled)	4 cups chopped

Meat and Fish:		
Meat	1 lb. cooked	3 cups diced
		2 cups ground
Chicken	5 lbs.	4 cups diced, cooked
Crabmeat	6½ oz. can	¾ cup flaked
Lobster	6½ oz. can	1 cup lobster meat
Shrimp	4½ oz. can	25 shrimp

Notes on Artists

Covers **Elaine Lewis Handy** studied graphic art and design at
and Cooper Union, the School of Visual Arts and with designer
Layout Alexi Brodovitch. A Rock Hill resident, she has worked for
over twenty years as an art director and designer for advertising agencies in both New York City and Sullivan County.

9 and **Shelley Doogan** of Lake Louise Marie has pursued her stud-
135 ies at the Art Students League since 1964. After a stint as a
textile designer in New York City, she moved to Sullivan
County and is currently gathering inspiration for her multi-faceted talent from the countryside around her.

21 **Lynne Berger** has studied at the Art Students League in
New York City since 1964. Primarily a painter, she has
worked as an illustrator and free lance commercial artist
since 1970. For the past four years as well, she has put her
talents to use at an educational film company in West-chester.

31 **Ethel Sipple**, a Roscoe resident and art teacher in Livingston Manor, has exhibited both in this area and New York
City. A graduate of the School of Fine Arts, Syracuse Uni-versity, she is known for her watercolors and oils which
have won many awards and hang in numerous private col-lections.

41 **Bud Wertheim**'s art training spans the globe, encompassing
schooling from New York University to the Sorbonne. A
practicing sculptor, painter, and silversmith for 30 years as
well as a teacher, this Livingston Manor resident has
exhibited in numerous cities throughout the U.S.

61 **Gretchen Hemming** of Woodridge divides her time and talents between commercial art, and painting and sculpting
where her preference of subject matter is wild life and
people.

67 **Isami Kashiwagi** born in the Hawaiian Islands, studied art
at the Pennsylvania Academy of Fine Arts. Also known as
"Sam, the Beekeeper", he devotes his energies to water-colors depicting the picturesque Mileses where he has
lived for the past ten years.

75 **Bob Longo** studied at Kutztown State Teachers College and
Columbia University. A Woodridge resident and art
teacher at the Fallsburg Central High School, he is an avid
watercolorist and photographer, and teaches at the Catskill
Art Society in Hurleyville.

81 **William E. Froelich** of Kenoza Lake graduated from the School of Fine Arts at the University of Buffalo. By vocation, an occupational therapist at the Roscoe Community Nursing Home and a consultant therapist at the Liberty Infirmary, Froelich devotes his free time to book illustrating for Graphos Studio.

89 **Peter Loewer,** a graduate of the School of Fine Arts at the University of Buffalo. Is both author and illustrator of gardening books. He is art director of Graphos Studio.

93 **Sylvia Mangold** received her training at Cooper Union and Yale University. A commuter from Callicoon Center to her teaching job at the School of Visual Arts in New York City, her paintings have been exhibited in over 20 group shows in the U.S. and at a one woman show at the Fischbach Gallery in 1974.

99 **Hazel Baum** of Monticello, graduated from Boston University, then took her talents to Harper's Bazaar magazine where she worked as a graphic-designer. In 1958, she was the winner of first place for "All Around Art" in Sullivan County, and continues to give expression to her talent in both oil and watercolor paintings.

107 **Billie Cohen**, a Monticello resident and horticulture student at the Bronx Botanical Gardens, studied Fine Arts at Pratt Institute. A recipient of various prizes and awards in student shows, she was the 1973 winner of "First in Show", at the Catskill Art Society.

117 **Jean Loewer,** a graduate of the School of Fine Arts at the University of Buffalo. Taught art in the public school system and in adult education classes. Presently working as a free lance illustrator. She is also teaching at the Catskill Art Society in Hurleyville, New York.

125 **Ann Higgins,** a free lance artist living and working in Sundown, graduated from the Rhode Island School of Design, majoring in textile design. She is also currently teaching art at the Liberty Elementary School.

157 **Alan Metz** of Fremont Center has applied his artistic talent as an illustrator of related science textbooks and as an art instructor at Brooklyn College. He has exhibited extensively in both group and one man fine art shows.

Inside front and back covers Photographs courtesy of **Jean** and **Mack Weiner** of Livingston Manor, from their collection of Early American household objects.

Contributors

Barryville:
Fran Ihlo
Jimmy McGough
Reber's Restaurant

Bethel:
Blanche Heller
Jackie Heller
Minerva Reinshagen
Claire Rettles

Bridgeville:
Old Homestead Restaurant

Bushville:
Jane Brodie

Callicoon:
Florence Curtis
Freda Molusky
Carol Roos
Kay Widmann

Claryville:
Marylin Barr

Cochecton:
Mary E. Bennett
Dorothy Schultz
Mrs. Wm. Shimpine

Eldred:
Eldred Preserve Restaurant

Fallsburgh:
Olympic Hotel

Ferndale:
Barbara Batinkoff
Beatrice Brender

Forestburg:
Elenor Osborn

Glen Spey:
Charnetsky Family
Glen Spa Restaurant
Mary Lou Karaim
Rose Labotsky
Mary Pasnick

Hankins:
Florence Herbert
Meredith M. Powers

Hurleyville:
Yetta Pohl

Jeffersonville:
Ted's Restaurant

Kiamesha:
Concord Hotel
Gibber's Hotel

Liberty:
Naomi Duchin
Duke's Restaurant
Grossinger Hotel
Doris Holmes
Muriel Jaffe
Ida Levine
Ann Levy
Singer's Restaurant
Helen Stamm
Hattie Zalkin

Livingston Manor:
Edgewood Inn
Vera Farrell
Carol Fehsal
Evelyn Haas
Janet Hinckley
Julia Ocenasek
Selma Spector
Slavia Mountain Resort
Jean Weiner
Alex Wittenberg

Loch Sheldrake:
Brown's Hotel

Mongaup Lake:
Judith Rhulen
Gloria Straut

Mongaup Valley:
Bert Feldman

Monticello:
Sunny Abramson

Monticello: (*continued*)
Florence Armstrong
Hazel Baum
Amy Berkowitz
Naomi Berkowitz
Lillian Block
Ivy Blumenfeld
Beverly Borwick
Rose Brand
Alan Brasington
Marcia Braunstein
Corinne Briggs
Lucille Budoff
Canton Restaurant
Chateau Restaurant
Charlie W's Restaurant
Billie Cohen
Lorraine Cohen
Shirley Cohen
Anne Coy
Agnes Dolan
Fredericka Dollard
Shula Drillings
David Drummond
Drew Durant
D'z Restaurant
Frances Effel
Edwin Field
Harriet Finklestien
Gustave Gavis, M.D.
Helen Gavis
Sally Gellman
Michelle Gersten
Ellen Golnick
Judith Green
Jeanne Greenberg
Grotto Restaurant
Alice Guttman
Margie Hornbeck
Shirley Hornbeck
House of Lyons Restaurant
Julia Jacobs
Macy Jones
Harriet Kaplan
Kaplan's Delicatessen
Barbara Katz
Sarah Katz

Michael Kouhana
Mildred Kreisworth
Eileen Kunis
Carla Kutsher
Kutsher's Country Club
Ann Lash
La Stella Restaurant
Erika Lauterstein
Jo Ann Lawler
Lefty's Charbroil
Mabel Lynch
Edith McClernon
Lorraine McCormick
Marcia McLaughlin
Gail Mittleman
Monticello Raceway Restaurant
Ellie Newman
Stephen Oppenheim
Paul's Potpourri Restaurant
Kay Pelton
Ceil Plotkin
Ruth Pollack
Dennise Rappaport
Leah Resnick
Ilene Rhulen
Roark's Tavern
Gloria Roche
Natalie Rosenbaum
Barbara Rubin
Mildred Seidler
Florence Sharkey
Florence Slatkin
Carrie Starr
Steak Pub Restaurant
Berdie Streifer
Ella Stuzin
Pat Taylor
Eva Topal
Lee Van Etten
Eugene Weinstein
Lenore Weinstein
Barbara Wells
Bea Wells
Mimi Wizot

Narrowsburg:
Century Hotel

North Branch:
Clemence Frank

Obernburg:
Ruth Brustman

Pond Eddy:
Anna Moch

Rock Hill:
Bernie's Holiday Restaurant
Elaine Handy
Jeanette King
Eva Klein
Nathana Rosen
Linda Schwartz
Sylvia Schwartz

Sackett Lake:
Ruth Patterson

Smallwood:
Joan Pailes

South Fallsburgh:
Marie Alberman
Florence Beytin
Brickman Hotel
Ruth Brizel
Jean Domfort
Carol Fein
Gilbert's Hotel
Herta Hauber
Pearl Lipson
Jo Maday
Molly Madnick
Shirley Malamud
Betty Maythenyi
Mary Oretsky
Pines Hotel
Raleigh Hotel
Frances Stratton
Windsor Hotel
Cookie Yacolino

Spring Glen:
Homawack Lodge

Sundown:
Ann Higgins

Swan Lake:
Stevensville Country Club Hotel

Wanaksink Lake:
Edna Hammond

White Lake:
Lighthouse Restaurant

Woodbourne:
Ruth Lachterman
Charlotte Rosenshein
Alice Scholefield

Woodridge:
Pauline Benton
Anna Cherviok
Angie Elliott
Barbara Friedman
Ruth Krieger
Naomi Leff
Irma Longo
Vera Meuhlemafeld
Ethelda Penchansky
Ruth Ruderman
Helen Salovin
Rose Schnall
Lillian Shabus
Vegetarian Hotel

Wurtsboro:
Noma Bocket
Calhoun's Catering
Happy Vineyard Restaurant
Florence Rothauser

Ellenville (*Ulster County*):
Celia Moshier
Dorothy Schlussel

Non-Residents:
Louise Bingel
Gretal Conal
Beverly Greenberg
Mary Loftus
Bertha Schraeter
Lillian Scolnick
Beverly Weinstein

Index